Do's and Taboos of
Public Speaking

Other books by Roger E. Axtell

Do's and Taboos Around the World: A Guide to International Behavior, 2nd edition.

The Do's and Taboos of International Trade: A Small Business Primer

The Do's and Taboos of Hosting International Visitors

Gestures: The Do's and Taboos of Body Language Around the World

Do's and Taboos of Public Speaking

How to Get Those Butterflies Flying in Formation

Roger E. Axtell

Illustrations by Mike Fornwald

John Wiley & Sons, Inc.

New York • Chichester • Brisbane • Toronto • Singapore

In recognition of the importance of preserving what has been written, it is a policy of John Wiley & Sons, Inc., to have books of enduring value published in the United States printed on acid-free paper, and we exert our best efforts to that end.

Copyright © 1992 by Roger E. Axtell
Illustrations by Mike Fornwald

Published by John Wiley & Sons, Inc.

All rights reserved. Published simultaneously in Canada.

Library of Congress Cataloging-in-Publication Data

Axtell, Roger E.
    Do's and taboos of public speaking : how to get those butterfiles flying in formation / Roger E. Axtell ; illustrations by Mike Fornwald.
        p.   cm.
    Includes index.
    ISBN 0-471-53671-7 (alk. paper)
    ISBN 0-471-53670-9 (pbk. : alk. paper)
    1. Public speaking.   2. Business communication.   3. Oral communication.   I. Title.
PN4121.A87   1992
808.5'1—dc20   91-42526

Printed in the United States of America

10 9 8 7 6 5 4 3 2 1

To the late John D. Davies,
a great speech coach.

And to Arthur W. Foster,
a great business speaker, mentor, and friend.

Acknowledgments

When we are watching the "Oscar" or "Emmy" award shows, the most *boring* segments of the evening occur when each honoree recites a whole list of names—people completely unknown to us—". . . without whom this night would not be possible."

I'd like to change that.

I'd like to try to breathe some life into those faceless names by telling you who aided in the writing of this book and what each contributed. Furthermore, each of the following is fully capable of writing his or her *own* book. So, in the future, you may want to be on the lookout for their names on the bookshelves.

Robert Williams is a speech writer, journalist, and president of his own public relations firm, Idea Associates Inc. Among his many credits are successful campaigns for dozens of state and federal legislators and at least one governor. He has also supplied the words and ideas that saved the necks of scores of business executives. Bob reviewed the entire manuscript of this book and offered helpful advice and anecdotes as well as encouragement and edits.

Mike Fornwald is art director at Arian, Lowe & Travis, a prominent Chicago advertising agency. Prior to that, he was a political cartoonist and then an animator for animated films. Mike supplied the wonderful illustrations throughout this book.

Peter Rosenberg is a marketing manager with a background in journalism who has also acquired special skills in the use of audio-visual materials in business presentations. Peter was responsible for researching and drafting Chapter 7, "Using Audio-Visual Equipment." He is a talented and personable young man headed for a successful career in business.

David Horwitz was a top television news executive for more than 20 years at CBS News, ABC News, and Group W. He produced award-winning broadcasts with Ted Koppel on ABC as well as the "CBS Evening News with Walter Cronkite" at CBS. David has converted this unique experience into a valuable consulting service that tutors business executives and others on TV appearances. David contributed substantially to Chapter 6, "Appearing on Television," with specific, memorable advice.

Phyllis Corbitt McKenzie, as you will learn in Chapter 9, "How to Turn Professional," is the founder and president of Capital Speakers Incorporated, a nationally known speakers bureau in Washington, DC. She works with hundreds of client companies and organizations in booking professional speakers from the ranks of business, government, literature, sports, politics, and entertainment. Phyllis provided substantial information for Chapter 9, a valuable contribution exceeded only by her personal charm.

Richard E. Rosenberg, a successful trial attorney, is now retired. He carefully reviewed and edited most of the manuscript for this book. When I became troubled by the enormous amount of time involved, his son explained, "Don't let it bother you. You've given him the three things he loves to do most: Work, help people, and criticize!"

Fred R. Holt is a former superintendent of schools, who was an outstanding debate and forensics coach. Fred kindly reviewed the early chapters of this book to assure that the principles being suggested were not only clear but correct. His solid "passing grade" was reassuring, to say the least.

Contributing in smaller but equally important doses were the following: Ron Dentinger, a stand-up comedian and banquet entertainer, who helped me with Chapter 5, "Humor"; the staff at the National Speakers Association who provided information on that organization for Chapter 9 as well as permission to reproduce data on NSA chapters around the country; Fred Knapp, of Frederick Knapp Associates, Inc., a college friend who has established his own national training and consulting firm for business executives in the areas of public speaking, media appearances, and image; and, Ron Dale, a delightful Scotsman and professional comedian who shared some wonderful insights into the art of humor.

My thanks, too, go to Steve Ross, my editor at John Wiley & Sons, New York City, who entrusted me with my last three book projects. Also, to Nancy Land of Publications Development Company, Inc., in Crockett, Texas, whom I have met only by telephone but for whom I have developed untold respect and admiration because of her special editing and design skills that magically turn typed words into a readable text. And she does it with a smile in her voice that actually warms the telephone.

Finally, I hope you will pause, if only briefly, at the Dedication for this book. The two names there represent a pair of admirable men who were blessed with special communication talents and who, throughout their lives, never hesitated to share them.

ROGER E. AXTELL

Janesville, WI

Contents

Introduction   **1**

1   The Three Secrets for Banishing Fear   **7**
When *Not* to Speak   11
Believe, Believe, Believe   15
The Third Rule   17

2   Organization of Business Speeches   **25**
The Art of Asking Questions   27
What Are the Six Magic Questions?   31
The Four Parts to Every Presentation   33
Timing a Speech   44

3   To Read, or Not to Read?   **47**
Writing for the Ear   48
The Art of Reading Aloud   52
Is It Fair to Your Audience?   53
When to Read a Speech   54
Tips on Using Notes   58

4   Getting Physical   **65**
The Eyes   67
The Voice   69
Gestures   72
Posture   73
The Lectern and Microphone   75
The Room   79

5   Humor   83

When *Not* to Use Humor   85
What Makes Humor Humorous?   87
Specific Examples   91
Humor to Bend, Borrow, or Steal   95
Roasts   101
Introductions   102

6   Using Audio-Visual Equipment   105

Which Medium for Which Meeting?   108
Which Audio-Visual Medium to Use?   110
Designing Visual Aids   113
How Visuals Are Produced   115
A Checklist for Your Next Audio-Visual
    Presentation   125
Room Preparation   127
General Tips   128
Summary   129

7   Appearing on Television   131

Where and How to Start   133
Nervousness   136
Clothing   136
Makeup   137
Body Language   138
Eye Contact   139
Gestures and Mannerisms   140
Selecting Your Words   141
Answering Hostile Questions   142
Other Types of Questions   144
In-House Video Presentations   146
Summary   147

8   Special Speaking Situations   149

How to Introduce Other Speakers   150
Serving as an Emcee or Moderator   153
The Question-and-Answer Period   156
Speaking to International Audiences   159

9   How to Turn Professional   **165**

How to Start   166
Marketing Yourself   169
Role of a Speakers Bureau   171
Fees for Professional Speakers   173
The National Speakers Association (NSA)   175
Other Groups   177

10   Resources for Help   **179**

General Sources   180
Toastmasters International   181
Dale Carnegie   183

11   Parting Advice from Successful Speakers   **185**

**Appendix   Local Chapters—National Speakers
Association**   **189**

Additional Reading   **193**

Index   **197**

Do's and Taboos of Public Speaking

Introduction

**What's in this book
for me?**

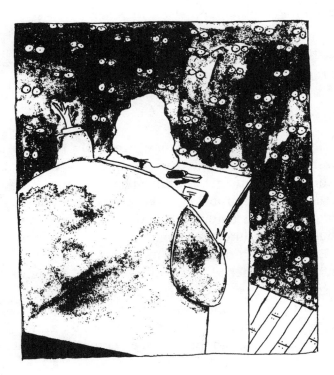

This book is intended for the businessperson who must speak to *any* audience of *any* kind, whether it be to the sales force, to stockholders, or to the Rotary Club; to the local city council, to union members, to the church membership, or to the corporate board of directors; or to a television reporter on camera.

Each of these occasions is a test of personal poise and business ability. And while this book will help you achieve poise and confidence when speaking to an audience, it may also produce some unexpected side benefits:

- *How to write a better business memo, letter, or report.*
- *How to read the newspaper faster and better.*
- *How and when to use—and not use—humor in business presentations.*
- *How to prepare for an appearance on television*—which may come about much sooner than you expect! (The reasons are explained in Chapter 7.)

Finally, some advice in this book may even stir up disagreement—even downright controversy—between different schools of thought on business public speaking.

Whatever the business situation, today's successful businessperson when speaking before an audience, must come across as intelligent, articulate, confident, and likable. Television comedian Bob Newhart once described the archetypical airline captain as "confidence personified, with straight teeth, crooked smile." And so it must be with the captains of business. They must appear before audiences as pin-striped Chuck Yeagers, the first test pilot to break the sound barrier and the model for every chief pilot since, complete with crooked smile.

However, many captains of business do not necessarily have that Yeager-like image. The reason is simple: In their career preparation and rise, most managers have just not taken the time to hone that important communications skill called public speaking.

Speaking before an audience is not easy. In fact, television programming has made it even *more* difficult. Now, by punching a remote control button, we have professional presentations costing millions of dollars per minute delivered instantly into our living rooms.

In the face of such competition, it takes a brave and well-schooled businessperson to dare to stand before an audience and maintain interest effectively. Still, it must be done; and in this day of "great communicators," public speaking is rising higher and higher among the coveted managerial skills.

The businessperson who is an effective public speaker will not only stand *out* but stand *above* his or her colleagues. He or she will also be a better motivator and manager of people, whatever the career assignment, simply because so much of good management today requires good communication skills.

This book, by itself, is not the magic potion for becoming a polished public speaker. As we quickly learn in Chapter 1, "To learn to play the flute, you have to play the flute." Translation: Nothing great is accomplished without actual practice, practice, practice. But this book does provide a road map to help the reader find more comfort, confidence, and competence in all types of business presentations.

The book begins by presenting "The Three Rules" that banish stage fright and provide the essential confidence for *any* business presentation. Then, in Chapter 2, the organization of a speech is taught, and as you'll see, it's as easy as adding 6+4, which happen to equal a perfect 10.

The natural temptation is to write out a speech verbatim and then stand up and simply read aloud what you have written. In Chapter 3, you will learn what's *wrong* with that method. One authority even calls it a way to "insult" your audience. However, many businesspeople are shocked, even angry at the thought that they should *not* read a speech verbatim, so this chapter could generate debate.

Chapter 4 deals with the *physical aspects* of public speaking: posture, eye contact, and gestures. Experts say more than half our daily communication is nonverbal, and so it becomes especially important to learn how to "get physical" when speaking to an audience. This chapter also offers numerous tips on turning lecterns and microphones into assets rather than impediments between you and your audiences.

In Chapter 5, you will learn not only about the role of humor but about the effective use of humor in your own public appearances. Numerous anecdotes and examples are provided to help you craft good openers, closers, and a few laughers in between.

Chapter 6 offers a short course on how to get the best from audio-visual equipment in support of business presentations. The days of using a few simple 35mm transparencies or slapping a couple of transparent films on an overhead projector are passing by quickly. Television has conditioned our eyes to expect slick multi media presentations. This chapter will teach you how to develop the audio and visual side of a business presentation, how to work with the technicians who prepare the visuals, and how to integrate all these elements into your presentation so smoothly that words and images are merged into memorable messages.

Next comes television. One young business friend told me, "I'll skip that chapter. I'm an accountant. I don't ever expect to appear on television during my business career." As you will read in Chapter 7, "Appearing on Television," the chances are close to 100% that, indeed, the experience of appearing on television will occur not once but many times in the career of any business manager less than 50 years old.

Chapter 8 offers advice on "Special Speaking Situations" such as the following: How to properly introduce other speakers, how to serve as a master of ceremonies or a moderator, how to handle those tricky question and answer periods at the end of every program, and how to speak to audiences of people from other countries.

Chapter 9 is designed for the business speaker who may want to consider branching out into speaking for fees. It is titled "How to Turn Professional" and details how to climb the ladder to professionalism. Business is the spawning ground for thousands of professional speakers—why not you?

Chapter 10 provides ideas for "Resources for Help." Here you will find ways to continue in your quest to improve business public speaking skills. Specifically, detailed information is provided on two national organizations that help train hundreds of thousands of businesspeople each year to communicate verbally with greater effectiveness.

The book concludes with Chapter 11, which offers some "Parting Advice from Successful Speakers." Some of these direct quotations might stick in your mind and may just help you make that jump from an average business speaker to an outstanding speaker.

The cartoon illustrations sprinkled throughout this book come from the talented pen of *Mike Fornwald*. Mike is art director at a large Chicago advertising agency and is a former political cartoonist and film animator.

Knowing that you are an effective public speaker can be a great source of pride and joy—and a distinct career enhancer. Unfortunately, few people in business today have discovered these truths. And with public speaking, as with just about every other skill, we all have our good days and bad days.

Yet, on one of those good days when you find yourself facing an audience that pays rapt attention to your every word, perhaps even nodding in agreement, and you finish your presentation with a final flourish, there is no higher plateau of satisfaction than knowing that you have achieved something both rare and enjoyable. That's when you feel as if you are flying higher than any jet pilot . . . and you can look out at the world and crack one of those confident but crooked smiles.

1

The Three Secrets for Banishing Fear

". . . the only thing
we have to fear is
fear itself . . ."

Franklin D.
Roosevelt

The *Book of Lists* has accumulated and ranked a dizzying assortment of fascinating topics. Among them is a list of humankind's worst fears. Is *death* our greatest fear? No. That's tied for only sixth place along with *sickness*. In fifth place, above *death*, is our fear of *deep water*. In fourth place comes our fear of *financial problems*. Third place marks our fear of *insects and bugs*, and second place, of *heights*.

What ranks as our *worst* fear? Even though our everyday act of talking is learned early in childhood, the prospect of talking to an audience, large or small, is branded as our worst fear.

It may be reassuring to learn that this preeminent fear is not limited to "ordinary folk." In the 1920s, one of the stage's brightest dramatic stars, Sarah Bernhardt, would upchuck before each performance. Today, celebrities such as TV weatherman Willard Scott and comedienne Lily Tomlin confess to powerful nervousness when stepping before the cameras. And, probably the greatest actor of our time, the late Sir Laurence Olivier, developed an almost disabling case of stage fright at the age of 60!

If, by chance, you happen to be one of those people who has never experienced this dreaded malady, count yourself among the celestially charmed.

The converse of fear is joy, and you can experience that, too, in speech making. Knowing that you have prepared and presented a nifty, well-received speech can generate a "high" fully equal to winning a championship sports contest, to receiving a public award or recognition, or to experiencing that flush of delight and well-being when your own child achieves some new goal.

On the other hand, if you have ever shaken hands with that old devil called stage fright, you can probably describe the encounter with the acuity of horror writer Stephen King: rapid, thumping heartbeat; quivering voice; a sudden moist, hot flash; a stomach that seems to be harboring a cold, alien being; and a mouth that tastes like an ancient, overflowing ashtray.

Why? Is it because of all those eyes staring back at you? Is it because an audience of your business peers seems to exude a cold air of expectancy that goes right for the throat? How can a superman or superwoman of business suddenly be turned into shivering jelly by merely ascending a platform and facing an audience?

Whatever the causes of stage fright, be assured it is no emotional weakness, no personality flaw. In fact, it is as common as a cold and as real as a quarterly earnings report.

Diverse solutions for overcoming stage fright can be found in scores of other textbooks. Those solutions range from deep breathing and other relaxation exercises to imagining that the audience sitting before you is completely naked.

All that practical and well-intentioned advice can be synthesized into three simple time-proven rules. Adopting these three rules will conquer the demons of fear. Practice this advice and the tension unwinds. Apply these three rules regularly, and your business presentation skills will begin to shine.

Before we examine those three rules, it is important to accept that a certain amount of fear (better to call it "apprehension") is not all bad. When speaking to an audience—any audience—it is *natural* to have some degree of tension. "Constructive tension" is what corporate executive and writer Richard W. Holznecht calls it. He is describing that upsurge of concentration, energy, and positive anxiety that football players feel when lining up for the kick-off. Sprinters do the same when putting their feet into the starting blocks. Observe Luciano Pavoratti in the wings before a concert. Even through the narrow eye of the TV camera you can see his body and mind tensing for the challenge. It can actually be a very exhilarating feeling.

Baseball great Lou Gehrig probably described it best. Late in his career, he was asked, "Weren't you nervous coming to bat in the ninth inning with two on and your team down 4–3?" "Of course I was nervous," Gehrig replied. "If I wasn't, I couldn't have hit that double off the wall."

"What you want to do," says Phyllis Corbitt McKenzie who heads Capital Speakers Bureau Inc., in Washington, D.C., "is to get all those butterflies in your stomach to fly in a planned formation" (Figure 1).

Figure 1   Get those butterflies flying in formation.

Now on to the three rules for vanquishing stage fright:

- *Know* your subject (in other words, "prepare").
- *Believe* in your subject.
- *Practice*, practice, practice.

On first reading them, they sound simple—almost mundane. But resist the temptation to say to yourself, "OK, those are easy enough. I can do that. I'll just jump ahead to the next few chapters."

Think about the first rule: *Know your subject. Prepare.* In that context, *let's apply Rule Number One itself*—and come to know *precisely* what is meant by those words.

WHEN *NOT* TO SPEAK

Many years ago, a mentor gave me this bit of homespun advice about life: "Buy low, sell high . . . and never walk behind a manure spreader."

The corollary is "Learn the value of good timing. And then, don't ever do anything stupid!"

Applying this advice to public speaking means: Know *when* to speak but also *when not* to speak. Speak *only* when you know the subject. *Decline* to speak if you are unsure about or unprepared for the topic. Otherwise, you may do something stupid . . . and end up walking behind that manure spreader.

Take calculus, for example. Teachers of calculus claim that a person can never truly *understand* calculus until he or she *teaches* it. To teach, a person must know. To know, a person must prepare.

As another example, one of my early English teachers drilled into us that we could not truly understand the definition of a specific word until we could define it *aloud* to someone else. And so it is with public speaking: Don't attempt to explain something aloud until you are fully prepared.

When accepting a speaking assignment, allow plenty of time to get ready. Research, plan, study, accumulate, sift, refine. It is better to decline an invitation to speak than to be ill-prepared and then speak poorly.

Listen to four successful executives:

- Robert Williams is a veteran public relations counselor to a wide range of corporate chiefs and has successfully managed dozens of political campaigns for governors and congressmen. "Ego so often gets in the way," says Williams. "When the chief exec should decline a speaking opportunity or delegate it to others, ego steps in the door and caution walks out. One result is bluffing. The boss is not fully versed on a subject and so policy can be made inadvertently from the platform. In fact, one day I plan to write a book about the egos of business CEOs. I plan to call it *My Daily Prayer: Lord, Deliver Me From Ego."*

- John Stollenwerk is president of Allen-Edmonds Shoe Company, a major manufacturer of quality shoes. John is a popular platform speaker at diverse business forums around the country because he dared to buy a shoe company during the 1980s at a time when more than 800 U.S. shoe factories closed their doors because of imports. He has turned Allen-Edmonds into a classic American success story. Stollenwerk's first and most important piece of advice for business speakers is simply "Know your subject." Your audience will quickly sense whether or not you are knowledgeable about your topic.

- Vincent Vinci, director of public relations for Lockheed Electronics Company, counsels that a solid presentation is based on three elements: Preparation. More preparation. Still more preparation.

- Serge E. Logan served as public relations director of the multibillion-dollar S. C. Johnson Wax Company, until his retirement in 1989. His job required him to (1) be the official spokesman for his company and (2) know his subject—Johnson Wax—as well as the original Mr. Johnson knew shiny, polished floors. When Logan traveled, he always carried two brief-cases: one for the presentation he was making at that time, and the other to carry office "catch-up" work. One morning, when leaving his hotel for the presentation, he inadvertently picked up the wrong case and arrived to find he had no presentation notes whatsoever. "I was told it was the best talk I ever gave," Logan said. "Thoroughly knowing your subject is the first key to successful business speaking—notes aren't necessary or even important if you're thoroughly versed."

The best salespeople in any field are, like Logan, the ones who know their product or their service: know it, live it, breathe it. Such intimacy breeds confidence and develops enthusiasm. Top sales performers like these can usually handle any resistance, objection, or question.

James H. Rich was the eastern regional sales manager for an internationally known consumer goods company who delivered hundreds of sales presentations to tough-minded buying committees for huge chains of retail stores in New York City. "The secret is in the preparation," Rich always advised. "When I prepared well, I did well. When I knew my material well, I was always more confident, more comfortable . . . and my audience could sense and see that immediately."

Knowledge of your subject defeats those fear-bearing demons. Knowledge breeds confidence and you actually become eager to relate your facts, to tell your story, and to illuminate your audience. You can avoid the following dreaded situations:

- Remember that lead-filled stomach when your class-room teacher, without warning, called on you for the answer to a question . . . and you didn't know the answer, or hadn't even been listening?
- What about the common nighttime dream that you are thrust on a stage. You seem to know something about the play but can't recall your lines? (No wonder evil spirits are pictured as hiding under the bed at night.)

While none of these scenarios is likely to happen in your company conference room, they dramatize that the best way to *experience* humankind's number one fear—speaking in public—is to be caught unprepared.

Speech consultant Robert Orben puts it succinctly: "Procrastination is the booking agent for stage fright." Orben is saying that if you delay *preparing* for a speech, it's like making a contract to guarantee fear.

Heavy preparation produces one other benefit, accord-ing to Bob Floyd, founder of his own giftware company: "I find that if I have an abundance of information and knowl-edge about my subject, I not only become more confident when I stand up to speak, but also that—because I am usually allocated only so many minutes for my presentation—I am forced to carefully *select* just the key and critical pieces of information. That makes my presentation more compact, more effective. The surplus data remain helpful in answering follow-up questions."

Don Aslett is the chairman of one of America's most successful cleaning firms and has more than 8,000 speeches behind him. Aslett has also written a book titled *Is There a Speech Inside You?* (Writer's Digest Books, Cincinnati, 1989). "I promise you," he writes, "that if you're prepared,

95 percent of the fear of speaking will leave you. (You need the other 5 percent to keep you humble.)" Aslett even cites the scripture: "If ye are prepared, ye have no fear."

With this corps of business professionals as testifiers, plus a venerable scripture for added import, I hope the simple-sounding words "Know your subject" have newfound meaning for you.

We now move to the second ingredient in the prescription to banish the fear of speaking: You must have *belief* in your subject.

BELIEVE, BELIEVE, BELIEVE

Nick K. was a reasonably successful sales executive in the Chicago area, but he had one significant weakness. When his company staged national sales conferences to unveil new programs for the next season, Nick would often disagree with parts of the new selling strategy. "It won't work. I'll sell it," he would say loyally, and then he would add, "but it won't work." Then, as Nick toured his territory with the new programs, *he would prove his prediction*.

What Nick lacked was *belief* in what he was selling. The result was a self-fulfilling prophecy that kicked into action and justified his prediction.

Have you ever watched evangelist Billy Graham on stage in a floodlit baseball stadium addressing thousands of followers? Is there any doubt that he *believes* in his subject?

Zeal is not limited to religion. Lee Iacocca's television commercials are probably the best contemporary example of the blunt, direct, "cut-the-crap" style of speaking. As with Billy Graham, there can be no doubt that Iacocca *believes* in what he is saying.

The late John Davies was one of the most successful speech coaches in the United States. He would always warn his students to "Never, never, never give a speech on a subject you don't believe in. You'll fail. On the other hand, if you have prepared properly, know your material, and *believe* in it . . . your audience will not only hear but *feel* your message."

Davies also counseled that proper preparation plus belief in your topic produces certain side benefits: Gestures become more natural, more automatic; the body is more relaxed, the mouth more lubricated, the voice steadier, and the eye contact more direct. (You will learn more about this *physical* side of speaking in Chapter 4.)

Now let's take these two pieces of advice—to prepare and to believe—and apply them to real-life situations.

Situation A

Let's say you or your management has just agreed to let the local Red Cross bloodmobile come to your company for a half day to collect plasma donations. Your job will be to address all the employees in your company on the subject of why donating blood is easy, painless, and important. If you were asked at that moment to step up to a microphone and present that information, two things would likely happen: (1) apprehension and fear would start to build, and (2) you'd probably flop. The reasons would be lack of preparation and lack of belief or conviction.

On the other hand, if you take the time to study all the available literature about donating blood, talk to the Red Cross nurses, and interview veteran donors of blood, then you are not only preparing but you are persuading yourself, "Hey! Donating blood *is* truly easy, painless, and important. Yeah! I can do this with confidence and comfort because I *believe* in it."

Situation B

Now shift to another real-life situation: You must appear before the Financial Committee of the Board of Directors of your company to present the case for a major capital expenditure in your division. The very same formula applies. Prepare and believe. Prepare by assembling all the facts. Prepare by asking questions—especially those questions a Board member might ask. Then ask yourself: "Am I truly convinced that this capital investment is warranted and necessary? Do I *really* believe it is proper and right? If it were my *own money,* would I invest in this?"

If you cannot convince yourself—if you lack belief in your message—how can you effectively inform and persuade others?

Remember Nick? He said the program wouldn't work, and he proved it wouldn't work. The same applies in *any* business speaking situation. Belief and conviction are contagious. And with them come two more attributes, enthusiasm and sincerity.

Business speech consultant Dorothy Sarnoff in her book *Never Be Nervous Again* (Crown Publishers, New York, 1987) describes this belief as a "spirit." She quotes the English poet John Milton: "A good teacher is one whose spirit enters the soul of the pupil." And then Sarnoff adds her own message on the power and the role of believing: "For me, a good speaker is one whose spirit enters the soul of the listener."

THE THIRD RULE

This rule—*to practice*—is as old as Aristotle, who wrote: "To learn to play the flute, you have to play the flute" (Figure 2).

You could read every book ever published on how to play the flute but wouldn't be able to blow a note without sitting down and actually playing, and practicing, the flute.

The same applies to any learning endeavor where you turn study into action: tennis, gardening, cabinetmaking, photography, poetry writing, skiing . . . and, of course, public speaking. In fact, try to think of an activity that does not improve with practice.

The other word for practice is "rehearsing." Marsha Lindsay, an advertising agency president, has a disciplined regime when preparing for a speech: "I try to rehearse so

Figure 2   "To learn to play the flute, you must play the flute."

much that I can give the speech with such ease and confidence it seems I am just up there talking, extemporaneously. I rehearse by not only practicing it silently, but also saying it aloud in front of a mirror and then into a tape recorder. I will also take the tape and play it, perhaps in the car en route to work, so that I can listen to my sequence of thoughts, my phrasing, my enunciation. Replaying the tape also helps implant the speech in memory."

Arthur W. Foster spent much of his business life training and motivating sales teams. He also presented quarterly sales programs to account executives for them to take into the field and present to thousands of customers.

Here was his step-by-step procedure for preparing a typical business presentation:

1. He began with research and, from that, decided on his basic message. Then he would "dump" all the raw material into one long, written rough draft. His purpose was to get all his ideas and facts laid out, albeit disjointed and unrefined.

2. Then Foster would carefully select attractive, memorable parts that were key to his message and covertly begin verbally trying them out on small, informal, unwitting audiences of friends and associates. He would do this to gauge reactions. In this process, he was also *rehearsing* the material by experimenting with different ways to relate the information.

3. Next, he would go back and convert the long first written draft into shorter, better organized, and proven "bites" of sound. Once again, he would start trying this revised version on fellow business executives, usually without their full knowledge of his purpose and, again, to gauge reactions and to gain more practice in voicing the messages.

4. As the speech became more and more refined, he would then start practicing it before a mirror (Figure 3). He would rehearse over and over, working on phrasing and timing. Not *reading* the speech, mind you. But, instead, *talking* it. During all of this, the words were being imprinted on his mind.

5. By the time the actual presentation time arrived, Foster had probably spent several weeks in preparation, had "auditioned" portions of the speech numerous times as insurance, and had presented the speech—aloud, for practice—at least a dozen times. The result? A polished, relaxed, convincing, entertaining, proven, and compelling message.

Figure 3   Practice, practice, practice.

If you consider Foster's method as long and laborious, Lockheed's Vinci tells of an entirely different, shorter, and more courageous approach. He tells of an East Coast company that established a "murder board" composed of knowledgeable and experienced managers who would listen to, and constructively tear apart the presentations of their fellow managers.

Which would *you* prefer? The slow, steady, deliberate method of developing and practicing . . . or the firing-squad version?

A more compassionate "audience" might be resting on your closet shelf: your portable video camera. It can be a wonderful supporting friend for practicing and rehearsing presentations. Set it up, start it running and do your stuff. In fact, the video camera has provided a marvelous new device to help us improve speaking skills. Consider these points:

- Until the advent of the video camera, the aspiring speaker had to rely solely on the critique of friends and associates. This was tough duty for both parties.

- The video camera is totally objective and serves as a mirror with a memory. Most of us are disturbed, even appalled, when first seeing ourselves on the screen. "Is that how I look?" we ask. "I didn't realize those lines in my face showed so much." When seeing ourselves on camera, we are usually harshly critical of ourselves. We often notice first what is unnoticed by an audience, and vice versa. While teaching public speaking to a class of business managers and recording each of them on camera, I had one woman executive become terribly flustered because, she said, "My hands look so ugly. I should hide them behind the lectern." That's what she had noticed first on the video replay. However, those in the audience quickly disagreed, saying, "No. Your hands are expressive. Don't change."

- On the other hand, until that same woman saw herself on camera, she did not realize that she was using *poor posture* when speaking. After seeing the videotape, she corrected it immediately. The camera was far more effective than if I, as the instructor, had commented "You tend to slump when you stand before an audience."

Incidentally, whenever you practice, try doing it in a situation that resembles the *actual* speaking situation as much as possible. In other words, if you will be making your presentation while standing, then practice it while standing. Similarly, if you will be seated for your presentation, practice delivering it while seated. If, for your actual presentation, your notes will be on a lectern, then be sure to place them at just that height when you practice. If possible, rehearse in the actual room where your presentation will occur. By all means learn if a lectern will be present. Better yet, *you* decide if you want to use one and place it where you will be most comfortable.

Does rehearsing pay off? Ask a President of the United States. Before any televised press conference, biographers tell us that Presidents and their staff meet routinely to work over "briefing books." These books contain every conceivable question that might be asked. Suggested answers and background information are provided. Then, the President rehearses likely answers over and over again.

In business, the same procedure is often followed when the corporate chairman of the board or the president prepares for the annual stockholders meeting. In many companies for weeks before this annual corporate rite, staffers are scouring *The Wall Street Journal* to cull questions that are being asked at *other* annual meetings. Also, they are looking for "hot topics" that might apply to their particular corporate situation and therefore might be asked by either well-intentioned stockholders or professional provocateurs.

As a result of this type of preparation, many corporate CEOs enter the annual meeting with a thick briefing book, tabbed according to likely questions, so that if and when a specific question is asked, the executive merely skims through the tab headings and flips to a well-prepared "spontaneous" answer.

Of the three rules presented in this chapter, this third piece of advice, to rehearse and practice, is probably the most important of all. The reasons are these:

1. You may *know* your subject, and you may *believe* in it, but all that can be ruined if you don't *present* it effectively. In sports terminology, this is what coaches call "execution." In other words, a football player may *know* the play, and he may *believe* that it will be highly successful in this situation, but if he does not *execute* the play smoothly, it can easily flop. No wonder football coaches require athletes to execute plays over and over and over again.

2. Rehearsing helps build confidence and conviction. After repeating one five-minute segment of your presentation three or four times, you'll find that soon you need only glance at one or two typed words or phrases in your notes and your mind will tell you, "Oh, yes, I know this section."

3. Rehearsing lessens fears. "The only antidote to that poison called stage fright," John Davies counseled, "is self-confidence . . . and the path to self-confidence is knowing and believing in your message, then bolstering that by having rehearsed and rehearsed again."

Practice does not always make us perfect . . . but it surely makes us better.

Apparently one of the greatest orators of our time, Sir Winston Churchill, agreed. One day, while the Prime Minister was splashing in his bathtub, his valet overheard him talking loudly. Believing he needed assistance, the valet entered and inquired, "Did you call, sir?" "No," Churchill replied, "I was just giving a speech to The House of Commons."

With these three critical rules in mind, the first and major hurdle to a successful speech—*fear*—becomes an obstacle no more. In fact, employ the basic rules of this chapter and you not only will go a long way to banish fear but will have the basic ingredients for *any* successful speech.

2

Organization of Business Speeches

**Six Magic
Questions + Four
Basic Parts = A
Perfect "Ten"**

I sure wish I'd done a better job of communicating with GM (General Motors Corp.) people. Then they would have known why I was tearing the place up, taking out whole divisions, changing our whole production structure . . . I never got all this across."

These apologetic words were offered by Roger Smith, Chairman of The General Motors Corporation, one of the largest corporations in the world. Smith retired in 1990, lamenting his failure to communicate effectively to his colleagues and employes during his 10 years at GM's helm. Smith presided over a near 10-point drop in the company's share of the U.S. car market, down to about 36 percent in 1989, and he said he feared GM would never regain the market share lost to rivals Ford and Chrysler.

Why? Why do CEOs of large—or medium, or small—U.S. corporations fail to communicate effectively?

In this day of the "great communicators," managers of businesses, large or small, must keep others informed. "Others" include business colleagues, employers, stockholders, the investment community, and government leaders.

This chapter deals with that vital business commandment "Thou Shalt Inform." In fact, another title for this chapter might be "Thou Shalt Inform Effectively . . . And Here's How."

We learned in Chapter 1 the three keys to good public speaking: (1) Know your subject. (2) Believe in your subject. (3) Practice presenting it over and over again.

This chapter will deal with *how to organize* a business speech—*any* business speech—so that you are *certain* to inform effectively. In fact, the lessons in this chapter will also help you become a more effective author of business memos, reports, and daily correspondence.

In this chapter, you will first learn about asking the *right* questions, because to inform, you must begin with questions. After that, you will learn the four basic parts to organizing any business presentation.

When you finish this chapter, you will be able to tackle a speaking assignment and organize it into a smooth, logical, and effective communications opportunity. Succeeding chapters will deal with the physical side of the speaking assignment: gestures, body language, use of audio-visual material, and humor.

THE ART OF ASKING QUESTIONS

Have you ever considered that the first statement ever uttered in the Garden of Eden might have been a question? As in, "Eve, would you like an apple?" (Figure 4).

Figure 4 Mankind's first question?

In business, the art of asking questions—especially the right questions—is respected, almost revered. There's much truth in the phrase "There are no dumb questions, only dumb answers." One CEO confessed to me that, when taking on new business assignments or projects, he would begin with this thought: "I not only don't know the answers yet, I'm not sure I even know all the necessary questions."

You do not have to search very far to find examples of the power of good questions:

> The time was Fall 1988. It was the third and crucial nationally televised debate between Presidential candidates George Bush and Michael Dukakis. Less than a minute into the debate, Cable News Network anchorman Bernard Shaw opened with a brutal question that many political analysts believe helped determine the outcome of the election. Shaw asked: "Governor Dukakis, if Kitty Dukakis were raped and murdered, would you favor an irrevocable death penalty for the killer?"

> Dukakis paused and, in a careful and objective manner, replied that he hoped justice would prevail. His answer made him appear cold and emotionless, upholding an image Democrats wanted him to shed. It may have been the single turning point in the presidential campaign.

Another example of the critical role of questions occurs every day in American courtrooms. Trial lawyers are trained and drilled on the use of questions. They are taught, "Never ask a question of a witness where you are *uncertain* of the answer." In other words, ask only those questions that will support your case. Avoid surprises.

Turning from courtrooms to business boardrooms, where surprises are also an anathema, the executive who is adept at asking good questions is a wise and usually effective manager. As I think back on 35 years in business, the two most able executives I ever worked for shared two admirable qualities: they were both good listeners, excellent listeners, in fact; and they both knew how to ask good questions. Through their questioning, they could drill right to the marrow of a subject. And, best of all, their questions would not reveal their particular biases or where they were heading in a discussion. Some of my colleagues, trying to interpret where these men were going with their questions, would often misjudge, try to jump aboard the boss's wagon, and find it heading in a different direction, leaving them sitting in the dust.

Whether you sell ideas or products, the process of selling has been described as the art of asking the right questions. Sales trainers and counselors teach that the purest form of selling occurs when the customer *convinces himself or herself* of the *need* to purchase the product or service. How? By the salesperson's asking a series of the right questions, which either elicit information that he or she can use to show how the product fills a need perfectly, or questions that steer the customer toward that same conclusion.

Here's a simple demonstration, a card trick that you can teach your children, but a trick that also demonstrates how the *right* questions can cause your audience to arrive at exactly the conclusion you want.

The Trick

The presenter stands before an audience, exhibits a deck of cards, shuffles them, and then holds the cards behind his or her back while asking these questions:

"There are, of course, four suits in a deck of cards. What are *two* of them?" *(Someone replies, "Spades and diamonds.")*

"OK. Which of those two do you prefer?"

(Someone answers, "Spades.")

"That leaves diamonds. What are three cards within the diamond suit?" *(Reply: "King, Jack, Queen.")*

"What are three more?" *(Reply: "Ace, two, three.")*

"What are three more?" *(Reply: "Four, five, six.")*

"Select two from the four, five, and six." *(Reply: "Five and six.")*

"That leaves the four of diamonds, doesn't it? How many cards do you want me to draw from behind my back before I come out with the four of diamonds?"

(Someone replies, "Six." The presenter draws six cards from his or her back and then, eureka! magically produces the four of diamonds.)

My father taught me that card trick when I was seven years old, so, as you probably suspected, the solution is not difficult.

The Solution

As you shuffle the deck in front of the audience, you surreptitiously note the bottom card before putting the deck behind your back. In the preceding illustration—and here's the whole solution—that card was the four of diamonds.

Through simple but adroit questions, you steer the audience to the conclusion *you wanted* all along: the four of diamonds. Now, knowing that your whole object is to steer the audience to the four of diamonds, here's how the right series of questions can accomplish exactly that.

When you ask "Name two of the four suits," if they reply, "Spades and diamonds" (as they did in the preceding illustration), fine, you are right on track. But, if they happen to say "Spades and *clubs*," your response is "That *leaves* hearts and diamonds, doesn't it?" *(Once again, a question.)* Naturally, your audience agrees. Ask them to choose either hearts or diamonds. If they say "Diamonds" you're OK, but if they reply "Hearts," you say, "So that *leaves* diamonds, correct?"

The same process applies right through the trick: "Name three cards in diamonds." If they name "King, Queen, Jack," just ask for three more . . . until they hit the desired four of diamonds.

You know that the card at the bottom of the deck behind your back is the four of diamonds, so you simply draw the excess cards from the top and then, finally, produce the diamond four after the number the audience has decreed.

Simple? All tricks are, once we know the answers. But the message here is more profound: Learn to ask the *right* questions to guide the audience to the desired conclusion or the product.

WHAT ARE THE SIX MAGIC QUESTIONS?

In the field of communication, the true professionals are journalists. They are trained to observe, ask questions, organize the results, and put them into words. "Good writing is clear thinking made visible" is one injunction in journalism.

The very first lesson budding journalists learn involves the Six Magic Questions: *Who? What? When? Where? Why? How?*

"Oh, that's nothing new," you say. "I knew those all along." Of course you did. But now that you are reminded of them, memorize them and begin to use them. Start using these six questions regularly when composing business letters, memos, reports, and especially when preparing for your business-speaking occasions. You will become a modern-day Moses, delivering that Eleventh Commandment for business: "Thou Shalt Inform." Let's put this proposition to a test. How do those Six Magic Questions inform effectively? The following is the first paragraph of a typical news story from a daily paper.

> MANILA, Philippines—Philippine jets and helicopters today blasted suspected military rebels battling President Corazon Aquino's forces for a second day in the strongest bid yet to topple her administration.

In journalistic terms, this is called the "lead," or the "lead paragraph" to a story. The purpose of the lead is to give the reader, right at the outset, the maximum amount of information in the shortest possible space. Let's see if the writer of the lead for this news story answered each of the questions:

QUESTION	ANSWER
Who?	. . . rebels battling president Corazon Aquino's forces.
What?	. . . blasted . . . rebels
When?	. . . today . . .
Where?	Manila
Why?	. . . to topple her administration.
How?	. . . jets and helicopters . . .

In a lead of just 27 words, the writer of the news story was able to answer all six questions and effectively inform the reader exactly what had happened that day in Manila. A journalist would continue the story by expanding on each of these pivotal points. Picture a pyramid: The lead is the tip, and each succeeding paragraph is a supporting layer of blocks.

With this lesson now in mind, you can begin to read your daily newspaper more effectively. As you scan your paper, read only the lead paragraph of each news story. From there, you can decide if you want to spend the time to read the rest of the article, which will only amplify that lead paragraph.

You should know, however, that this rule does *not* apply to newspaper *feature stories*. It applies only to straight news stories. Feature stories are a different form of writing because they usually pertain to human interest subjects and are more anecdotal, whereas a news story is relating specific information about a specific event.

We digress into newspapers, lead paragraphs, and methods for reading your daily paper more effectively because this exercise provides important evidence that answering the Six Questions is the most effective single way to inform people on any subject. (Note that we have dropped the word "Magic" because, in truth, it really isn't magic anymore . . . it is just good common sense.)

Remember the lesson to be found in your daily newspaper:

Most business presentations are intended to inform. If your objective is to inform your audience, you should assure that your material is organized so as to answer the Six Questions: Who, What, When, Where, Why and How.

How many business meetings do you attend each week? One consulting firm in business communication conducted a nationwide survey of almost 500 companies and learned that executives in those companies were attending more and more meetings, and liking them less. More than 70 percent of the respondents labeled the meetings "a waste of time," and 89 percent said the meetings "lacked advance planning and organization."

You can avoid these criticisms by organizing your material properly. Borrow from the journalists and other writers. Ask yourself good questions about your topic. Do your research. Then make certain your presentation provides answers to the six basic questions you've now memorized.

From crucial *questions*, we now turn to critical *parts*. There are four basic, fundamental parts to every business presentation.

THE FOUR PARTS TO EVERY BUSINESS PRESENTATION

A familiar quotation in public speaking is from an unknown country preacher who said: "How do I organize a good sermon? Very simple. I start by telling 'em what I'm going to tell 'em. Then, I tell 'em. Then, I tell 'em what I told 'em." Good advice. The preacher's homespun logic applies to business presentations, also. We'll come back to those wise words later.

The *four* parts of any business presentation have simple, innocent-sounding names, but each one could deserve a separate textbook:

- The Headliner.
- The Opening.
- The Middle.
- The Closer.

You should organize your remarks into these four basic compartments no matter what the occasion in business speaking (Figure 5).

The Headliner

Think of a headline in a newspaper. Are you aware that there are specialists, artisans in every newspaper room, who are

Figure 5   There are four parts to every business presentation.

absolute masters in arranging just the right words in the smallest spaces? Using a half-dozen words or less, these headline writers capture the essence of a complex event that may take a thousand words to describe or explain in detail. Like most artists, they learn it through constant practice.

So it is with business public speaking. James R. Peterson, former president of Pillsbury and later executive vice president of R. J. Reynolds, says he begins preparing for every speaking occasion by asking, "What is my headline?" This headline is not the *title* of your presentation, but it is a short description of your whole objective for the presentation, as in the following example.

> The marketing vice-president of a huge consumer goods company offers this real-life experience: "For many years, we customarily equipped our sales representatives with beautifully printed and crafted portfolios containing the current seasonal program. Our salespeople were supposed to visit the head buyers at each of their accounts and go through the portfolio, often page by page. But if you've ever been in a buyer's office, you know that it is often small and cluttered and the buyer is impatient and harried. We learned that more and more of them would just brush aside our beautiful portfolio and demand that the salesperson 'Just tell me what the basic program is.'"

Using this example, how do you, the business speaker, develop your "headline"? How do you determine that "basic" message? You begin by taking the lessons from Chapter 1 (know your subject, believe in it, and practice) and combine it with the lesson of the first part of this chapter: Be sure to answer Who, What, When, Where, Why, and How.

Now ask yourself: "What is the 'headline' for my presentation? What phrase, thought, or conclusion do I want my audience to hear, to absorb, and to take away with them?"

> Let's use that example again from Chapter 1 where you must address all your employees to urge them to donate blood when the community bloodmobile visits your office. In this

case, your headline might be along these lines: "I want my audience to clearly understand that giving blood is quick, easy, virtually painless, and a wonderful humanitarian act.

Marketing counselor David L. Weiner puts it this way: "You have a message. It is important. You want every member of your audience to leave the room with that message clearly in his or her head. Now, ask yourself—what is *my* message, stated in the shortest possible sentence or paragraph?" Brevity is important: If *you* cannot synthesize or boil down your message into a single, elementary statement . . . how can you expect your audience to leave the room with it firmly fixed in mind?

Charles Osgood, TV anchor on CBS, confesses that he often writes the *last* line of a speech *first*. Since the last thing you say is what your audience is most likely to remember, that should be your basic message.

The CEO for a giant Midwestern firm prefers to think in terms of a "magic pill." He says, "When I want to communicate something to my audience, I think how nice it would be if I could simply encapsulate my message into a small pill. Then I think of having my audiences swallow the pill and instantly absorb and comprehend my message. But then—and here's the challenge—I ask myself, 'Exactly what is the message I want crammed inside that particular tiny pill?'"

Still another trick is to imagine your business audience streaming out of the room after your speech. Suddenly, a few of these people are confronted by a researcher who says, "Quickly, in as few words as possible, what message did you receive from the presentation you just heard?" Then, imagine the respondents saying, "Well, what I heard in that presentation is . . ." Ideally, you would hear the message in your "headline" or the ingredients of the magic pill.

The headline is important not only because it ensures your audience's comprehension but also because it then becomes the spinal column for *organizing* the body of your speech. Almost every other part of the speech should complement and support that single message.

Now let's turn to those other basic parts: the opening; the middle; the closer.

The Opening

Roger Ailes, the top media and speech advisor to President George Bush, has advised, "In the first seven seconds (that you meet people), you shower your audience with subtle cues."

Try it yourself next time you are in an audience. We all tend to size up a speaker in less time than it takes a sprinter to run once around a track. How does the speaker appear? Strong? Nervous? Confident? Eyes averted? Smiling? Frowning? Tall and straight? Apologetic? Bright-eyed? Slumping? Clear-voiced? Formal? Relaxed?

Take consolation, though. Audiences *want* a speaker to succeed. They don't want you to fail, or stumble, or to be embarrassed, because audiences empathize with speakers. Audiences don't like embarrassment any more than you do. They are hoping that you will be confident, smooth, clear, and concise.

The first few moments of any speech provide your opportunity to signal all those positive attributes. Just like an Olympic sprinter who gets a powerful start "out of the blocks," the opening of your presentation sets the pace for the rest of the speech. It is for this reason that it is wise to pay special attention and preparation to the opening.

The standard, universal opening is "Good Day, ladies and gentlemen," usually followed by "I am glad to be here today." In highly formal situations, protocol often requires that you address each dignitary in order of importance: "Senator Johnson, Mayor, Madam President, Reverend Tompkins, ladies and gentlemen."

Avoid both these openings. They are trite and boring. Instead, jump right in and surprise your audience.

Here are specific tips for your opening:

- Step to the front, pause, look around at your audience, and smile. A smile is universally understood.
- Then, wait a few beats, until you have the audience's attention. There is no faster way to get an audience to turn their attention to a speaker than 5 or 10 seconds of silence. This is also a good time to take a few easy, rhythmic breaths.
- You should have rehearsed your first words well in advance. Use the standard "Good Morning" if necessary, but avoid the cliches: "I'm glad to be here" or, worse yet, "A funny thing happened to me on the way here."
- Another old chestnut is to begin with apologetic remarks about being "not qualified" or "not prepared." Speech writer Robert Orben writes that he always cringes when he hears those phrases. Orben says he is inclined to think, "Well, if you're not qualified or prepared, why are you wasting my time?"
- American business speakers often begin a presentation with a joke or anecdote. Chapter 5 in this book deals with humor, so if you plan to open with a touch of humor, be certain to review that chapter.

The opening need only take one minute, or three, or up to five if necessary, but it should accomplish the following:

1. Establish you as a relaxed, likable person who sounds knowledgeable and competent.
2. Intrigue or amuse the audience.
3. Present a summary of your message, or headline. "Tell 'em what you're gonna tell 'em." Explain the purpose of the meeting, or the purpose of your presence.

First Example

One polished CEO speaker opened his presentation with this true story:

> I have a friend who gives speeches in Japan. He uses an interpreter. So my friend speaks a sentence or two and the interpreter translates—back and forth. We found out later that *this* is what the Japanese interpreter *actually* said: "American is beginning speech with thing called joke. *(Pause)* I don't know why but all American businesspeople apparently think it is necessary to begin speech with joke. *(Pause)* I won't tell you joke because you won't understand it. *(Pause)* He thinks I'm telling you joke now. *(Pause)* Polite thing to do when he finishes is to laugh. *(Pause)* I'll tell you when he finishes. *(Pause)* He's getting close. *(Pause)* Now!" Well, the Japanese, being such a gracious people not only laughed, but they stood up and gave my friend a standing round of applause. After the presentation, my friend approached the interpreter and said, "I have been giving speeches in this country for 10 years . . . and you are the first interpreter that knows how to tell a good joke!"
>
> Well, this morning I am *not* going to open with the standard business joke. Instead, my purpose here this morning is . . ."

Second Example

Former Governor Lee Sherman Dreyfus of Wisconsin would never travel to a city in his state for a speech without first having a member of his staff phone, several days ahead, to collect information for his opener. The staffer would spend several hours collecting tidbits of information: recent events in that city, who would be present at the event, who would be seated at the head table, problems existing in that city, who should be honored or congratulated, and so on. From this information, Dreyfus would be better prepared to craft his opening to include numerous local touches. Also, his opening would show his audience that he knew what was happening in their community and that this was not just another canned speech.

Third Example

Public relations counselor Robert Williams gets his audience involved right from the starting gun with a "snap quiz." When he speaks to executives on the subject of political power sources, he produces a list of special-interest groups: Bankers, big business, prolife, prochoice, teachers, physicians, union members, and so on. Then he asks: "Which is the most powerful political force on this list?" After a well-timed pause, his answer is invariably a surprise to his business audience. "In our state, the most powerful political force is the 27-year-old, energetic teacher of your children at your local school. The reason? Because he or she is part of a 48,000-member teachers' union who all volunteer to stuff envelopes, knock on doors, and become educated on the issues." It is, first, the involvement of his audience and, second, the surprise answer that provide Williams with his unique opener.

Work hard on the opener. Don't read it from a prepared text. Try it out first on friends and family. Say it aloud privately over and over again until you can repeat it smoothly, only glancing at a note or two if necessary. Make certain it achieves the preceding objectives.

The Middle

Probably the greatest orator of this century was Sir Winston Churchill. In his biographies, we are told that Churchill's rule of thumb was *one hour* of work and preparation for every *one minute* of a speech.

Churchill's messages rank with the most important in this century. He knew that the "Middle" of any spoken presentation is the true heart of the message. This is the very reason you are standing in front of the audience: to deliver information or inspiration or to seek a decision.

Thomas Russo manages a successful investment firm in New York City, and each week he finds himself addressing audiences of highly placed business executives. "My formula," Russo says, "is to have four basic points—no more than that. My Harvard Business School professor taught me that, and over the years I've found that he was absolutely right. An audience can usually only assimilate four points, not many more. So they become the all-important middle part of my talks. I have an opener, a closer and in the middle I have my four points."

If your mission is to inform, the middle is where you impart the *answers* to the Six Magic Questions.

To prepare for the middle, do the following:

- List the key points you have assembled for your message.
- Arrange the points in logical order. Remember in school when you learned how to make a written outline? You had major headings designated by Roman numerals, and subpoints under each heading. Do the same thing here. Or, try drafting a table of contents for your speech.
- Check your notes to make absolutely certain your outline conveys your headline.
- Go back over your outline and begin to expand methodically and explain each key point. Use examples, stories, and images to fortify each point. Don't be afraid to repeat a point by using different examples or anecdotes.

Now begin thinking about another important element in the middle: *transitions*—statements that help you carry the audience smoothly from one major point in your outline to the next.

Transition statements, as in the following example, are also extremely useful in reminding the audience *where you are* in your outline.

> Now that we have learned *what* blood plasma is and *how* it is used to save lives, let us turn to this matter of actually giving the blood. I want to describe now exactly what happens when you enter the bloodmobile so that you will understand that this wonderful act of giving can be virtually painless . . . actually enjoyable.

Did you spot the good preacher's advice to "Tell 'em what you told 'em"?

Transition statements are extremely important in spoken presentations. In a written text, the eye can quickly jump backward to remind the reader of earlier points, but an audience cannot do that as easily with the spoken word. Therefore, you, the speaker, must constantly *remind* the audience where you are in your outline.

If the headline is the spinal column of your presentation, then the middle is flesh and bone. The audience now begins to see the body of your message.

The Closing

You have now reached the last few moments of your presentation: the finale.

In the theater, you always save your best for last. In musicals, for example, this means saving the most outstanding music or dance number for the finale. In dramas, the last act delivers the climax or the memorable concluding lines or messages.

The reason for finales and climaxes is so that the audience leaves the theater with strong, positive memories. Playwrights and producers want playgoers turning to one another as they file out the doors murmuring, "Wasn't that wonderful!" So it is with a speech.

In the closing, it is always wise to *summarize*. Quickly summarize the key points of your whole presentation using a few memorable words or phrases.

Try to close your speech with a "doozie." That's the same as having an ace in your hip pocket (Figure 6). It's your best

Figure 6   Keep an "ace" in your hip pocket for the closer.

line, your most dramatic point, your most profound thought, your most memorable bit of information, or your best anecdote—but *only* if it supports and strengthens your headline. Playing that ace at the right moment will make you a winner.

As with the opening, work hard on the closing. Practice it aloud, over and over again. Be able to repeat it smoothly, without stumbling. Never mind that you may not say it precisely the same way each time—you don't want it to sound stilted. Instead, just make sure that the message, the emphasis, and your sincerity are all present. Many speakers make the mistake of "swallowing" the last few words of a speech: Be absolutely certain that your last few words are delivered slowly, clearly, and with conviction.

After you've delivered your "doozie," look at the audience, smile again . . . and sit down.

TIMING A SPEECH

"There is no such thing as a 5-minute speech," many professional meeting planners and managers frequently lament, frustrated with speakers who are asked to make a 5-, 10-, 15-, or even 30-minute presentation, and who invariably take longer.

The reason for this common complaint is that many business speakers don't organize and practice their speeches and just don't take the effort to time their remarks in advance, thus losing track of time. If you wish to stand above the crowd, you will, while practicing and rehearsing, glance at a clock or watch and observe how many minutes it takes you to complete the presentation.

Some experienced speakers actually consider it a blessing if, while rehearsing, they find their speeches slightly longer than the allotted time. "That forces me to cut out weak and superfluous parts," one of them confided. "It also boosts my confidence, because when the time comes to deliver my talk, I realize I am delivering the best parts of my research and preparation."

Here is another trick concerning *timing:*

> Luxury cruise ships often engage what they call "enrichment lecturers" to provide programs for passengers. During a cruise, one of these speakers, a retired businessman, became acquainted with a professional comedian who was part of the ship's entertainment staff. The businessman asked the comedian to observe his lecture and offer constructive comments on how to improve style, delivery, posture, and so on.
>
> After the first lecture, the professional said: "You were fine, but I have one suggestion for you. I noticed that you frequently looked at your watch. Now, I realize you probably did that because you did not want to go beyond your allotted time. However, it's a proven piece of crowd psychology that when a speaker glances at his watch, many in the audience do likewise. This becomes both an interruption and a distraction. The audience becomes aware of the time elapsed when they should be concentrating fully on the speaker's remarks."

The lesson here is to avoid looking at your watch. Instead, place your wristwatch on the lectern in advance. Or, better yet, observe a clock in the back of the room. If you're very lucky, the lectern will be equipped with a digital clock.

If you have been assigned 20 minutes for your talk, note the exact time as you arrive at the lectern and tell yourself "OK It is 1:15 PM now. I *must* finish when the clock says 1:35." In this way, when the clock reads "1:30" you will say to yourself, "I've got 5 minutes. I should be nearing my conclusion about now."

Being sensitive and conscientious about timing is a boon to everyone: The meeting organizers will love you, the audience will stay interested and not become restless, and because you have taken the time and effort to *organize, practice,* and *time* your talk, you will be more confident and effective.

3

To Read, or
Not to Read?

> ". . . the written
> word and the
> spoken word are by
> no means the
> same . . ."
>
> **Norman Thomas**

Peggy Noonan is a professional speech writer who has written speeches for both former President Reagan and President Bush. She is credited with providing the phrases "Read my lips" and "A kinder, gentler nation," which became synonymous with President Bush in the first two years of his administration.

The very existence of speech writers like Noonan causes many businesspeople to think that if they just hire a good speech writer, they will become memorable speechmakers overnight. Unfortunately, that assumption is dead wrong.

Speech writers are valuable both in politics and in business. They can capture abstract ideas and put them into practical language. But they cannot make their clients great, or even good, business speakers.

In fact, many speech consultants suggest that if at all possible, *avoid* reading a speech.

"What?" you exclaim. "What about the President of the United States? What about all those people you see on TV at the United Nations? What about the Annual Stockholders' Meeting? My CEO always has a prepared text that she carefully reads word for word. If there is that corps of hotshot speech writers who do nothing but *write* speeches, a lot of important people *must read* them. Why isn't this a good idea?"

WRITING FOR THE EAR

The answer is that there is a distinct difference between writing for the *eye* and writing for the *ear*. Professionals who write for the print media—authors, journalists, poets, speech writers—know that writing for radio or television requires a completely different style.

Here's why:

- Printed words allow the eye and mind to do the work. Readers can refer back to an earlier sentence, skim ahead for key points, and retreat to read a complex passage.
- But the ear hears only one word at a time. The listener is at the mercy of the speaker, who doles out words like puffs of smoke (Figure 7).
- Information we obtain through reading and listening is stored in our memories differently. In printed material, the eye and mind can jump from passage to

Figure 7   An audience only hears one word at a time—then the words disappear into the air.

passage, and then circle back and review. With the spoken word, the memory can retain only bits and pieces of information, moving forward without an opportunity to review, and therefore the listener often has trouble recalling what was said a few moments earlier.

- As a result, writers who write for the ear quickly learn to use shorter sentences, active verbs, and simple grammar and syntax. They also learn to repeat basic thoughts, cloaking them in analogies or anecdotes to make a more memorable impression. They avoid words that are difficult to pronounce, obscure words, or phrases that do not flow easily off the tongue.

- Another difference is that we can read with the eye considerably faster than we speak. The average speaker talks at a rate of 100 to 120 words a minute. We can read and think at a rate of about 800 words a minute, while we can listen at a top rate of 400 words a minute. So, as speakers talk, a listener's mind is racing up, down, and around, and occasionally coming back to absorb the speech. Even the most exciting speaker won't hold everyone's complete attention: It is estimated that people listen intently for only 3 seconds out of each 10-second segment while their minds wander for the other seven seconds (Figure 8).

- Truly accomplished speech writers provide a rhythm and pace and lilt to their language. They can employ special word devices such as "parallelisms," a favorite technique of the late President John F. Kennedy, who offered one of the most legendary parallelisms in his inaugural speech: "Ask not what your country can do for you; ask, instead, what you can do for your country."

Ms. Noonan was a skilled speech writer because she knew and practiced these principles. In her book, *What I Saw*

Figure 8 People listen for only 3 of every 10 seconds, while the mind wanders for the remaining 7.

at the Revolution: A Political Life in the Reagan Era, (Random House, New York, 1990), Noonan said: "I began my career writing for the ear. I learned how to write for broadcast, how to be conversational and catch the listener's attention, how to try to sum up a situation with a good, true line."

Such speech writers try to enter the persona of the person they're writing for. Speech writers are first and foremost professional listeners. Then they translate their client's speaking style into written words.

Most businesspeople are *not* experienced in writing for the ear; in their daily letters, memos, and reports, they are accustomed to writing only for the eye.

As a result, they are inexperienced and ill-equipped to write for the ear, as professional speech writers can do. This is the first reason people in business should not write out a speech and then read it verbatim to an audience.

THE ART OF READING ALOUD

The second argument for *not* reading a speech is that most business executives have never had training in *how* to read aloud.

- When reading to an audience, eye contact is limited. (We'll learn more about the importance of eye contact in Chapter 4.)
- When reading aloud, it's easy to stumble over words and run the risk of getting lost in the text. Pages can also get mixed up, and you can become easily flustered trying to get back on track.
- Reading aloud often sounds monotonous unless the speaker has practiced pacing, rhythm, modulation, and emphasizing the nouns and active verbs in a sentence.
- Good, experienced readers sound as if they are *talking* to the audience, not reading. You can see this skill in action every evening: Watch the national news anchors deliver the evening news, and remind yourself that they are reading from a teleprompter. Peter Jennings, news anchor on ABC, is reputed to be the best of these professionals. Watch him to observe how natural he is, even though he is reading every word.

I learned this lesson firsthand when I worked at a local radio station in high school and college, and also as a writer and announcer for a weekly national network radio show in Chicago. I learned there is an *art* to reading words aloud and making them sound natural, interesting, and convincing. Famed sportscaster Red Barber confessed he always pretended he was in the hallway talking to just one person rather than reading sporting news to hundreds of thousands of people across the United States.

Radio announcers also learn certain disciplines early in their careers that businesspeople rarely consider. For instance, announcers must never go back and *repeat* a muffed phrase. The reason is that it just calls more attention to the mistake. I learned that the hard way when reading a commercial for swim trunks: "Be sure to get your smart fighter trunks at Anderson's clothing store." But I got the words "smart fighter" mixed up, transposing the sounds of the first letters. I said "fart smighter" and then realized frantically "That didn't sound right!" In my inexperience I then committed the cardinal sin: I *repeated* the mistake. Finally realizing what I had said—twice!—I blurted out "Oh, I mean 'smart fighter' trunks," which caused our listeners to realize exactly what I had said the first two times around. The telephone complaints, and the laughs that followed, quickly proved to me that there is an art to reading a prepared text aloud that most people lack.

IS IT FAIR TO YOUR AUDIENCE?

The *third* argument for not reading a speech is probably the most compelling of all. It goes back to the two keys to making successful speeches: Know your subject, and believe in your subject. Reading a speech can imply to your audience that you don't truly know your subject.

Clarence B. Randall, the late chairman of Inland Steel Corp., a powerful and popular business public speaker, argued that reading a speech verbatim was tantamount to insulting your audience. He claimed that if you didn't know your subject well enough to stand up and "give it to 'em right from the shoulder," then you shouldn't be up on a platform in the first place. Others argue that the speaker who feels he or she must *read* an entire speech might be better advised to simply *hand out the written text* and let the audience read it quietly and at their leisure.

Can you imagine a professional salesperson sitting down in front of a customer and *reading* his or her sales pitch? The salesperson might say, "Oh, you interrupted me. Now I've lost my place."

Next time you attend a meeting with multiple speakers, compare the effectiveness of one speaker who *reads* a prepared text with another speaker who stands up and *talks* to you, the audience. Which speaker is most enjoyable to listen to? Which is more believable? Who is more motivating and inspirational?

Sometimes, with highly complex subjects, it is necessary to arm the audience with charts or tables of figures. In ordinary presentations, however, it is deadly to distribute materials or the text of a speech in advance. When that is done, the average person in the audience naturally starts scanning the text, flipping pages, and sprints well ahead of the speaker's slower, spoken words.

These are all the arguments for *not* reading a speech. *But there are exceptions.*

WHEN TO READ A SPEECH

There are, obviously, occasions that justify reading a speech verbatim. Here are some of them.

- When your words must be absolutely correct or accurate, and you cannot possibly risk an accidental misstatement. Such occasions might be when you are responding to lawsuits, commenting on potentially explosive subjects, or making a statement to the media and don't want to risk being misquoted.

> Melvin R. Laird was a Republican congressman from Wisconsin, majority leader, and later Secretary of Defense. When he campaigned for office, he never read a speech—his style was friendly, direct, and conversational. As Secretary of Defense, he was required to read his speeches; but during the question and answer sessions, he came alive again and, because of his earlier training, spoke extemporaneously handling questions superbly. In fact, when Laird retired, the press corps presented him with a gold football standing on a wooden platform. The inscription read: "Mel Laird 239—Capital Press Corps 0." The significance was that in 239 press briefings, the reporters had never once caught him unprepared, lying, or fudging. He *knew* his subject, was *prepared*, and years of *practice* paid off.

- Another occasion that often requires reading from a prepared script is the presentation of slides, transparencies, or other visual aids when another person is controlling the projection equipment. Then, obviously, both the speaker and the aide must operate from a written script. Even this can be circumvented, however, by the use of a "clicker" or some other signal to indicate the operator should move to the next slide.

- Finally, a third situation that may dictate the use of a written text is when time and pressure simply do not allow for rehearsals or advanced preparation; or when you must present several *different* speeches in one day to different audiences.

Since 1986, I have had the privilege of serving as a part-time, dollar-a-year advisor to the governor of Wisconsin. As part of my duties, I contribute ideas or phrases or complete texts for speeches. Our governor usually works from a prepared written text, for several reasons: (1) He may speak several times each day on different subjects to different audiences, (2) he cannot afford to be misquoted, and (3) he wants the media to have a written record of his comments. In his case, through years of accumulated experience, he has become an accomplished reader. But he admits he feels more comfortable and more effective when he can depart from reading a text and speak directly from his mind and heart.

If you absolutely must read your speech, here are some tips to help you be more effective.

1. Always *practice reading the speech aloud.* Try to practice in a setting similar to the actual setting of your proposed speech. For example, if you will be using a podium and lectern, then practice standing and reading from a podium. (This is an especially important tip if you wear *bifocal glasses* because some lecterns are positioned at a height just out of focus of your lens.) If you will be appearing in a large room, practice in a large room. If you will be using a microphone, practice speaking into a microphone so you can become acquainted with the amplified sound of your voice.

2. Keep as much *eye contact* with your audience as possible. When you look up from the text, don't look just straight ahead; make eye contact with the people on the left, on the right, and in the center. If you have read the text aloud over and over again, looking up will become much easier. Maintaining eye contact is also easier if you use short sentences and paragraphs. Also, as you read, practice jumping ahead with your eyes to read the *end* of a sentence, which is usually the most important part of the thought. Then, while looking up at your audience, say those words.

3. *Listen to radio and TV announcers,* especially newscasters. They are professional readers. Listen to how

they use inflections, pauses, and modulation. Note that they sound as if they are talking, even chatting, with you. Newscasters use pauses as a form of punctuation to add emphasis. They also have excellent enunciation and articulation. The untrained reader/speaker usually lacks many of these traits. We also tend to read *every* word instead of using contractions, as we do when we talk. For example, the script might read "they are"; but when talking, we'd say "they're." As a result, when reading aloud, most of us tend to sound stilted instead of relaxed. Novice radio announcers learn to read effectively by pretending they're having a conversation with just one person instead of reading into a microphone to hundreds or even thousands of people.

4. Prepare your written text in the following format:

   - Use large type and double- or triple-spaced lines.

   - Use short sentences and short paragraphs.

   - Repeat important thoughts often.

   - Use a three-ring binder instead of loose pages that can become shuffled and mixed. An alternative is to use cards: The 5-inch by 7-inch cards are a popular size. The advantage of cards is that they are firmer than paper and make less noise when shifted around.

   - Leave plenty of white space at the bottom of each page or card to help you keep your head and eyes up, looking out toward the audience as much as possible.

   - Leave extra white space on the left-hand margin of the page as well. That way, if you are not using a three-ring binder, you can slide the top page to the left and quickly move your eyes to the top of the next page.

   - Use a wide left-hand margin to write short reminders to yourself such as "Slow down here" or "Smile" or "Strong emphasis here."

5. Allow your voice to rise and fall to provide variety, and slow down when you want to emphasize a point.

6. Don't forget to smile.

7. When drafting a written speech, follow the same rules for *organization* as for any other speech: the Six Magic Questions plus the Four Basic Parts.

8. Finally, don't forget the key lessons in Chapter 1:
   - Know your subject.
   - Believe in it.
   - Practice, practice, practice.
   - Turn to your friend the video camera to practice your delivery and especially to assure good eye contact with your audience.

An alternative to *reading* a speech would be to *memorize* it. I would suggest you avoid trying this unless you have an absolute fail-safe memory. With memorization, you run the risk of forgetting part of your speech and finding yourself staring at a room of confused people.

If reading a speech is at one end of the spectrum and memorization is at the other, and both are to be avoided, what lies in the middle?

TIPS ON USING NOTES

The obvious and preferred middle ground between memorizing and reading is to prepare *notes* (Figure 9). Why are notes preferred over a full, written text or over memorization? There are several reasons:

- You want to be able to step before an audience with *confidence* and present a well prepared, well practiced, memorable speech. The skilled speaker should be able to talk than read his or her speech. Keeping a

Figure 9 Take only a few, well-prepared notes to the lectern.

short set of notes can be like buying an insurance policy to help you succeed.

• Notes help you *remember* all the parts of the speech you spent so much time preparing. Even the most polished speakers can have memory lapses. I once attended a "Speaker's Showcase" sponsored by a state association of speakers. The purpose of the showcase was to allow a parade of professional speakers to "audition" or demonstrate their services before an audience of meeting and program managers. One of the speakers was sailing along smoothly when she suddenly stopped smack in the middle of her presentation. She went "blank": that most dreaded of all speakers' nightmares. The poor woman almost dissolved into a puddle. If she had discreetly placed a short outline or a small set of cards somewhere nearby as a refuge, she might have avoided this calamity.

- Written notes are memory joggers, confidence builders, and a "security blanket" all in one. They help you display the relaxed confidence and competence that is vital to a skilled speaker. They allow you to maintain good eye contact with your audience, and increase your sincerity and believability.

How should notes be organized?

I have surveyed dozens of speakers with this question and the conclusion is this: *It depends entirely on the personal preferences and whims of the speaker; there is no single preferred format.* Here are some ideas you may want to adapt to suit your own speaking style.

Former Wisconsin Governor Lee Sherman Dreyfus, who is now a full-time professional speaker, prefers 3-inch by 5-inch cards on which he writes or types short phrases or thoughts. One card may represent two to five minutes of speaking. In his case, his notes are memory keys that unlock the door to a familiar and well-practiced anecdote or to a series of ideas. The cards might contain a quotation or an abbreviated paragraph, or even a single word. These short bites of information can keep you from sounding stilted or unnatural, as reading complete sentences often does. This technique also forces you to look up and out at the audience. Another advantage to Dreyfus's system is that he can shuffle the cards around, changing the order or inserting new ones, depending on the audience and the message he wishes to convey at that time.

Another speaker I interviewed prepares a broad outline of his talk in large-size type. "I keep the headings short—sometimes just a word or two—so that all I have to do is glance at them and they'll unleash the longer passage of words I want to present," he explained. "An outline like that does two things for me. First, it assures I'll move logically from point to point; in other words, that my presentation is organized. And second, I know that I'll avoid 'going blank' right in the middle because if I should become temporarily lost, all I do is glance down and quickly find my place."

Herbert J. Grover, State Superintendent of Public Instruction for Wisconsin, prefers a less formal format. He simply carries a handful of news clippings, notes, cards, and other assorted records to the podium with him. By following the sequence of his assorted collection of notes, he is able to move smoothly from point to point in his presentation. He needs no other reminders.

For my own speeches, I use *handwritten* outlines, with the "key word" technique. I also use different colored inks to help me differentiate one point from the next. I always write my outlines by hand because, first, taking the time to carefully write down each key word and phrase also helps further implant the message in my mind. Second, the different colored inks allow my eye to quickly locate the major blocks in my outline. I also use key phrases and never write out complete sentences.

For example, one after-dinner speech I present around the country is based on a guide to international behavior I wrote called *Do's and Taboos Around the World* (John Wiley & Sons, New York, 1990). The following is my message, or headline: *To succeed in international business, American businesspeople must be more sensitive and aware of the different behavior and protocol around the world.*

Here are my actual notes for the *opening* of that speech:

- Dais
- Savoir-faire
- "Very American"
- Japanese interpreter
- Our topic today

In actual presentation, these nine written words represent about four minutes of verbalization. They also represent hours of preparation and practice so the speech can be presented in a relaxed manner. For me these few notes are also sufficient to instill confidence that I won't stumble or falter or forget *exactly* what I want to say.

What do those words represent? Here's how those few notes translate into spoken words:

"Thank you, _____. Let me say at the outset that I am very leery of this arrangement up here. I don't like these platforms that many hotels provide . . . you know, they're called a *dais*. I spoke in Buffalo, New York, two months ago where we were seated on a raised dais like this. The presenter gave me a very nice introduction, turned to me, and said, "And now here is our speaker, Roger Axtell." I buttoned my coat, pushed my chair back and *fell backward right off the dais*. I looked like Greg Louganis doing a complete backward one-and-a-half somersault. Well . . . the others on the dais rushed to my aid and I could hear the audience gasping—and laughing—but I'll be honest with you. All I could think was "My gosh, now I've got to get up and *talk* to this bunch."

(This is a true story, incidentally. Because it's true, it's easy for me to remember and relate it. More on that subject in the chapter on Humor.)

(I then explain that if I'd been a polished speaker, I would have quickly recovered, brushed myself off, and simply said to the audience, "Well . . . how do you like me so far?" But, I add, I didn't have that savoir-faire so prized in business around the world.)

(This transition allows me to tell another true story about the definition of the term savoir-faire, a story that I have practiced and know audiences enjoy.)

(After that story, I then explain:)

What I have just done here in the past few moments is something peculiar to American business . . . *very American*. (I then tell the story about the Japanese interpreter for an American speaker in Japan. We American businesspeople have our own set of customs and behavior, such as always beginning a speech with a joke, and we forget that our customs are not shared by other business groups around the world. See page 39 for the full version of this story.)

(That consists of my opening. I have told three, true, amusing stories and also explained to the audience what the topic of the speech is about.)

(The next "block" of notes in my outline is written in another ink color. In my case, the new color tells me that I've finished the opening and now am moving to the middle.)

Remember that this is just *one* way of preparing notes. You'll develop your own style—the one that works best for you—as you make more and more speeches.

4

Getting Physical

"Delivery is more
important than
content."

Arch Lustberg,
speech trainer.

Sixty percent of our communication is *nonverbal*, according to well-known social anthropologist Edward T. Hall. That means whenever we stand before an audience, our stance, our posture, our facial expressions, our hand gestures, our whole body dynamic communicate more than our actual spoken words.

Teacher and coach John Davies always counseled his students to remember three specific actions when speaking: "Stand up so you'll be seen. Speak up so you'll be heard. And then sit down so you'll be appreciated."

A stiff, immobile speaker is often a boring and usually ineffective speaker as well. It is therefore essential to know how to be physically relaxed, which will allow your actions to complement your words.

In this chapter, we will start at the top of the body with the eyes and move down: voice, gestures of hands and arms, and posture. We will also examine other aspects of this physical side to speaking: how to make the microphone and lectern your allies, and how to turn the entire physical arrangement of the room into an asset instead of a liability.

First, two important definitions: A *podium* is the raised platform at the front of the room where speakers stand to deliver presentations; it is also called the *dais* (pronounced *day-us*). The stand used to hold notes is called the *lectern*. A lectern can be a short stand placed atop a table, or it can be a free-standing unit with a light, microphone, and sometimes a clock attached. The terms podium and lectern are often interchanged and misused, and for that reason, the skilled speechmaker should know this distinction.

THE EYES

Within many cultures around the world, it is believed that the eyes are the windows to the soul. In public speaking, since we usually want to arouse both spirit and soul, the eyes become the most important physical equipment of all.

Start by thinking about one-on-one conversations. Have you ever conversed with someone who kept looking away constantly, avoiding eye contact? This behavior often illustrates discomfort or dishonesty. Conversely, the person who maintains good eye contact is displaying sincerity, attention, and respect.

The single most important physical action in public speaking is to have direct eye contact with your audience (Figure 10).

Some instruction booklets on public speaking suggest you can avoid nervousness by looking out over the heads of your audience. That may relieve nervousness, but how would you feel if you were conversing with your boss or a subordinate or a customer and they kept staring at some spot just above your head? This behavior becomes not only disrespectful but irritating to your audience.

How can you practice and learn good eye contact?

To answer that question, let's refer back to the analogy used earlier in this text about learning to play the flute. You can *read* everything there is to know about the flute, but the only way to learn to play it is to actually do it. Therefore, the only way to cultivate good eye contact is to practice doing it *each time* you speak.

Here are some helpful tricks:

- Be aggressive. When speaking, pick out a specific pair of eyes in the audience and bore right into them, for just a few seconds. Then move over to another set; do the same, and on and on.

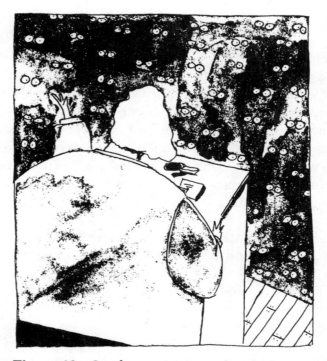

Figure 10   Good eye contact is the single most important physical action when speaking.

- Don't allow your eyes to jump around helter-skelter. Do it with purpose. Look left. Make a statement. Look center. Make a statement. Look right. Make a statement. Look at eyes in the back of the room. Make a statement.
- Each time your eyes move, pretend to yourself that you are talking only to that individual.

I have interviewed a number of skillful business speakers who told me that with these techniques they have been able to recapture the attention of a temporarily disinterested listener. When experienced speakers spot one person in the audience whose eyes are looking down or off at another part of the room, they issue a concentrated dose of words and look directly at that person. This can actually coerce the distracted listener to reestablish eye-to-eye contact with the speaker.

A business manager whose job is to conduct frequent tours of his factory explains his technique of gaining eye contact (and attention): "As I look from person to person, trying to gain direct eye contact, I often spot someone—usually in the back of the group—who is not looking back at me. I find that by singling out and directing my remarks directly at that person, I often get him or her to refocus on what I am saying."

Here's another experiment to measure the level of interest of *any* given audience. Position yourself at the back of a room during a series of presentations and simply watch the heads of the audiences: If they are all tilted up, looking toward the speaker, it is usually indicates the speaker is being effective. On the other hand, if a good assortment of heads are looking downward or sideways, the speaker is losing his or her audience. (The only exception to this rule is if people in the audience are diligently taking notes.) This trick even works *within* a speech. When presenting dry, complex facts or statistics, odds are that the eyes and heads will stray. But, if you raise your voice, pound the lectern, or tell a story about real people and real events, the odds are that you'll turn heads back in your direction again. A good speaker communicates with the audience with his or her *eyes*.

THE VOICE

The first person to discover he didn't like the sound of his own voice was probably Thomas Edison. When he invented the first phonograph, he heard his own historic words, "Mary had a little lamb." Like most of us, Edison was probably disappointed because our voices sound different on a recording and we usually don't like the result. The reason is that our voices sound better inside our heads than they do when played back on recording machines.

The two important lessons here are (1) Your voice probably doesn't sound as bad as you *think* it does, and (2) if you are troubled by the sound of your voice, there are simple ways to improve its quality.

Nervousness is usually the culprit affecting the quality of our voices. Voice consultant William Rush offers three easy ways to relax and thus upgrade your voice:

1. *Slow Down.* As with driving a car, control is easier at slower speeds.

2. *Release the Upper Body.* "Take a breath, rotate your shoulders, relax your neck," Rush says. All these actions will create more relaxed vocal chords and make your voice sound deeper and more pleasant.

3. *Take Breaths from Your Stomach, Not Your Chest.* Short breaths reduce vocal quality. Breathing deeply from the diaphragm allows a richer, more relaxed sound.

In addition, for effective speechmaking, *avoid the monotone voice.* The worst vocal outpouring is a monotone. By every measurement, a flat and unvaried ribbon of sound is uninteresting and grating. It is no accident that "monotone" is the stripped-down version of "monotonous." Therefore, another way to improve your vocal delivery is to vary the pitch. Here are some hints about pitch and modulation to remember:

- When we want to convey something very important and serious, we all tend to talk in a *lower tone* (and, incidentally, at a *slower* pace.)

- In ordinary conversation, we speak in the mid-range between bass and treble.

- And when we are excited or a little silly, our voices creep up to the higher range.

Use these natural conversational habits in your speeches. The main goal is to vary the sound of your voice, and to have the pitch and modulation complement your delivery.

Accents

Do Southerners or "New Yorkers" have an advantage or disadvantage? Rush's rule for answering that question is as follows: ". . . I don't mess with it unless the accent will hurt a person's credibility or render him unintelligible. For example, when someone with a down-home accent tries to sell stocks in a metropolitan area, the accent might not help."

Laughter

This may surprise you, but as a speaker don't be afraid to laugh, where and when appropriate. Laughter is a wonderful sound. And it's contagious. Have you ever noticed how professional comedians such as Johnny Carson occasionally join in the laughter following their own jokes? When a speaker laughs at the right moment it can make the audience feel good.

Dry Mouth Syndrome

A dry mouth obviously hinders good voice quality and is a direct result of nervousness. Here are three ways to minimize the dry mouth syndrome. First, instead of sipping cold water, which tends to tighten the vocal chords, take a hot drink instead. Warm liquids tend to relax the throat and vocal chords. Second, try to force a yawn. Strange as it seems, yawning tends to stimulate salivary glands and relieve that terrible dryness. Third, if neither of these works, as sometimes happens if you are taking a medication that causes dry mouth, ask your pharmacist to supply an over-the-counter liquid spray solution that creates an artificial saliva, providing temporary relief.

GESTURES

Many decades ago, in the old schools of oratory, speakers were actually drilled on how to make six or seven basic hand and arm gestures. For example, accompanying the statement "The accused sits . . . *there!*" you envision an orator directing a dramatic accusatory finger at the defendant. Or, in scratchy black-and-white films from the past, politicians may be seen smacking a fist into their palm as a means of pounding home a point. Finally, picture a speaker with hand raised head high, index finger pointing stiffly upward and you can almost hear the words, "There is one, and only one issue at stake here."

Happily, today we don't have to learn such gestures by rote. There is a much easier way. Listen, again, to the words of speech coach John Davies:

> If you *know* your subject thoroughly, and *believe* in it with your heart, I have good news for you. Gestures will become automatic, almost instinctive. Then, the only self-tutoring you need to do is study yourself on videotape to sort out the weak gestures from the strong ones. You'll see them, don't worry.

What are examples of "weak gestures"?

- Fiddling with your spectacles.
- Playing with a pen or paper clip.
- Reaching in your pocket and unconsciously jiggling the change there.
- Repeatedly patting your hair, scratching your head, pulling on an ear, buttoning and unbuttoning a coat.
- Frequently clearing your throat.
- Using any single gesture over and over and over again.

Why are these bad? In a single word, they are *distracting*. They distract the audience's attention from your message.

On the other hand, strong, forceful, and complementary gestures strengthen your presentation. When Lee Iacocca pounds the desk with his fist, his words take on special meaning. When the Reverend Billy Graham points his finger at the TV camera, we get the clear message that he is speaking directly to us. Gestures should be physical actions that fit and support the words.

If you harbor any doubts about the role of gestures and body language as we communicate, read the book *Manwatching*, by Desmond Morris (Harry N. Abrams, New York, 1987). Morris shows, with a variety of illustrations and excellent observations, how every body motion is also a signal. He also demonstrates how famous historical personalities used hand gestures just as a symphony conductor uses a baton to communicate to an orchestra.

In short, if you speak with conviction and take the time to watch yourself on videotape, you'll be able to sort out and discard weak gestures and replace them with stronger ones.

POSTURE

A company CEO approaches the lectern to speak at his company's annual shareholders meeting. He is a tall man, so he towers over the lectern. He then places his hands and arms stiffly on either side of the lectern, hunches over his notes, and begins reading his remarks.

His strong voice issues one message but although the CEO doesn't realize it, his body language strongly suggests he is hanging on to the lectern for support. Further, he hovers over his speech like a huge bird of prey covering its kill with outstretched wings. With his head down, he rarely looks up at his audience, suggesting he is not really interested in them. Advisors to this CEO will confess privately that he dreads the ritual of the annual meeting. He cannot wait to finish his speech. To perceptive people in the audience, his posture clearly reveals all his discomfort.

In contrast, observe a well-prepared CEO who is confident of her remarks and is anxious to tell her story. She walks to the front of the room, smiles at her audience, and with a relaxed manner begins her comments. Her posture will usually reflect all these attributes.

The video camera will reveal if you are guilty of any of the following postural taboos:

- Slouching or hunching over the lectern.
- Repeatedly bouncing on your toes or rocking back on your heels.
- Keeping head and eyes down, rarely looking up.
- Clenching hands tightly together.

Some speakers employ a special walking technique. Try walking a few feet away from the lectern to address one side of the audience; then walk to the *other* side to make another point. This walking movement brings you closer to the audience, provides visual variety for them, and is also a physical way to signal a relaxed transition from one point to the next. Here's how it might work:

> *(You are delivering a speech on the merits of donating blood, standing in the middle of the stage, with or without a lectern, and you say)* "Giving blood can be a very satisfying and rewarding act that is really simple and painless at the same time."
>
> *(Now, turn to the right, walk a few paces in that direction, and say)* "Knowing that you've perhaps saved the life of another human can warm your own heart over and over again. It's probably one of the most humanitarian acts you can do in your daily lives."
>
> *(Then, turn back to the left, take a few steps, and address these remarks to the people on your left)* "And the time it takes is only minutes—less than an hour. Furthermore, your friends

and colleagues who have donated blood before will be the first to tell you that it is really quite simple and painless . . . actually enjoyable."

This walking technique helps insert your whole body into your presentation and can be developed with a little practice. It requires good timing and must be practiced carefully so that it looks natural, but it can be an effective way to use your body to punctuate and underscore your remarks.

THE LECTERN AND MICROPHONE

The average speaker ascends a dais, moves to the lectern, taps or adjusts the microphone, clears the throat, and then remains rooted there for the rest of his or her presentation.

In contrast, the person who wishes to be *above average* will do the following:

- Before the audience arrives, inspect the room to assure everything is in place: lectern, microphone, and any other audio-visual equipment that you'll need.

- Check the height of the lectern; many are adjustable. The lectern should not be so tall that only your head shows, nor should it be so low that it is difficult to read your notes.

- Check the audio-visual equipment to assure that everything is operating properly and that you know how to turn lights on and off, change slides or transparencies, and even change a light bulb quickly if the one you are using happens to burn out just before or during your presentation. Most important, if you are using a remote control unit for a slide projector, get thoroughly acquainted and rehearse with each button. I have seen speakers in the middle of their presentation accidentally begin pushing the "reverse" control instead of the "forward" control, continue reading from a script, and create total confusion between words and images on the screen.

- Pay special attention to the microphone. So many speakers step up to the microphone, adjust the "gooseneck" holder (which always creates an ugly, grating sound), and then begin to speak not knowing if the voice is booming or barely being heard. Another tipoff to the skill and experience of speakers is to note if they clear the throat or, worse yet, if their first words are "Can you hear me?" It is far wiser to check out the microphone well in advance, assuring that the volume level is set so that people in the back of the room can hear you comfortably. Remember, too, that a room with an audience absorbs sound, so if you test the microphone in an empty room, boost the volume slightly to compensate for the audience. In such cases, the sound technician responsible for the audio system can become your best friend; ask him or her to check out the system with you before your presentation.

- If you are suspicious that people in the back of the room may not be hearing you, here's a smooth, professional way to handle it. Just say: "Please help me with a speaker check. If you can hear me in the back of the room, raise your hands." That enlists the help of the audience and tells you quickly and efficiently exactly what you need to know.

- Inquire if someone is available to monitor the volume control for the microphone and be prepared to make adjustments while you are speaking. This is especially helpful if "feedback"—that loud screeching noise—should occur. Feedback can happen almost everywhere, no matter how advanced or professional the sound system or the setting might be. It develops when the sound reaches a volume that actually "feeds back" the speaker's voice through the microphone. The only way to stop the resulting assault on the eardrums is to lower the volume level.

- Be careful of standing too close to the microphone. The result, in radio lingo, is called "popping your P's." Every time you use a word beginning with the letter "p," the microphone picks up that little explosion of air from your lips and it comes through the system sounding like a pistol shot.

- Observe where the microphone cord is located, especially if it snakes along the floor to the side or behind the lectern. More than one speaker has tripped over that cord on the walk across the podium.

- Try moving *out and around* from the lectern. Skilled speakers know that the lectern can represent a barrier between a speaker and the audience (Figure 11). That's why many novice speakers stand rooted behind it, often leaning on it for support. The lectern becomes both a prop and defense barrier. But, if you observe experienced speakers, you'll notice they will move from one side of the lectern to the other as if signaling that they are anxious to make better contact with the audience. Some will also stand at the side and casually put one elbow on the side of the lectern, presenting a friendly, relaxed pose to the audience. When using this technique, here are some tips:

- Be careful not to step out of range of the microphone.

- You may want to arrange in advance to be equipped with either a hand-held microphone, or a "lavalier" mike, which hangs around the neck or clips on to the lapel. The latter offers extra freedom to move out from behind the lectern and also frees up the arms and hands for more gestures.

Figure 11   Don't let the lectern become an obstacle between you and your audience.

- Another type of microphone is a "remote" mike. There are two styles: A cordless battery-operated microphone, and a miniature microphone that clips to the tie, blouse, or coat lapel with a wire leading to a portable power pack that clips to the waist.

If you are still dubious about how the lectern represents a shield and obstruction between you and the audience, start observing the altars of modern churches, stages for TV award programs, and the podium arrangements used by professional seminar leaders. In each case, the speaker either operates without a lectern, or the lectern is a transparent stand. The reason, as we have learned here, is to avoid having the speaker partially blocked from the audience and to allow the speaker to use the full body.

THE ROOM

Many veteran speakers I have interviewed say that they always check out the room where they will be speaking well in advance of their presentations, to get familiar with the setting and to anticipate any potential problems.

For example, one of the *most difficult* room arrangements for a speaker is when the audience is spread out a full 180 degrees from left to right. In this situation, the tendency is to look straight ahead, virtually ignoring the two thirds of the audience to the left and right. In such cases, it is better to make the extra effort to include the *whole* audience in your eye contact, addressing some statements to the left, other comments in the middle, and still more remarks to the people on the far right even though you'll have the feeling that you are turning the back of your head to part of the audience.

Here are some other factors to look for when examining the room where you'll be speaking:

- How far is the lectern positioned from the audience? Sometimes it is thoughtlessly placed 10 or even 20 feet away, leaving a physical gulf between you and the audience. In that case, ask for the lectern to be moved forward so that you will be physically closer.

- Where will you be seated prior to your introduction? What path will you take to walk to the podium and then to the lectern? Must you walk from the back of the room, or through people seated on chairs? Must you ascend a podium? (If so, check the height. There is no worse overture to a speech than falling flat on your nose just seconds before you are supposed to speak.)

- If possible, place your notes on top or on a shelf of the lectern in advance, rather than carrying them with you. Having your notes already in place on the lectern is a small touch that avoids having to carry them up, lay them on the stand, and play with or shuffle them. This technique, however, is not foolproof. I did that once and the speaker before me inadvertently carried my notes away with him. I arrived to find . . . nothing! (One solution is to place your notes *underneath,* on the small shelf usually located within the lectern.)

- The *worst* of all room settings is a small audience seated in a large room. Speaking to a small group in the ballroom of a hotel is intimidating to everyone: The speaker is distracted by all the empty space and the audience is reluctant to relax or become involved with the speaker. The only ways to counteract this are (1) try to encourage the audience to come and sit closer together down in front, and (2) try to position yourself as close to the audience as possible. The objective is to reduce, as much as possible, the potential barriers between you and your audience. Conversely, when an audience completely fills a room, the speaker is buoyed because so many have come to hear his or her message, and the audience's response is often better: Laughter and applause seem to be freer, almost contagious.

- Here's something most speakers ignore: Where are you supposed to go when you *finish* your remarks? Do you sit down on the dais? Do you return to the audience? Are you supposed to retreat to the back of the room? Determine the answer in advance by checking with the program organizer.

5

Humor

"We are all here
for a spell; get all
the good laughs
you can."

Will Rogers

83

The phone call usually comes in the late afternoon. It's from a friend who says "I'm giving a speech tomorrow. Do you have any good jokes for me?" It's a natural thing to do. I've done it myself. In business-speaking situations, we almost always want to be entertaining as well as informative, and that translates into opening with something humorous. But waiting until the day before your speech for a guaranteed, surefire funny line is as dangerous as diving in the dark.

To determine how best to use humor, I've done a great deal of research on the subject.

Here are the results of this research:

1. Being a humorous speaker is not easy. Like anything else, it takes work and practice.

2. What may be funny depends on two factors (1) the nature of your audience, and (2) how the joke is told (i.e., timing).

3. Anecdotes and funny stories rarely come along at the very last moment. They require disciplined research and then practice.

4. It *is* helpful, in spite of all these obstacles, to incorporate humor into your different presentations. The reason is simple: People like to laugh. As babies, we learn to laugh before we learn to talk. As adults, we know that laughter releases curative endorphins into the body. Furthermore, audiences tend to like people who can make them laugh, and if audiences like you, they will listen more carefully to what you say.

Humor plays an important role in business. *Forbes* magazine found in a 1987 survey that 98 percent of 737 chief executives interviewed would hire a candidate with a good sense of humor over a humorless type. Further, a researcher at California State University at Long Beach, David Abramis, studied 341 workers and found that those who had most fun at their jobs were more likely also to be the most productive. Why? Because having fun reduces mental tensions, discourages conflicts and boredom, and increases creativity. Even the Talmud teaches that a lesson taught with humor is a lesson retained.

"Humor does more than release tensions and evaporate hostility. It also opens up channels to others, shows us how to communicate clearly and reminds us when we aren't communicating," claims psychologist Herb True, in his book *Humor Power* (Doubleday, Garden City, NY, 1980).

Media researchers at Indiana University discovered that children learn and retain better when entertaining material is interspersed with serious content. Business trainers use humor to build rapport with attendees in their classes and to underline key learning points.

This chapter will examine the role of humor when making business presentations, as well as how to use humor effectively.

WHEN *NOT* TO USE HUMOR

In 1978, I was scheduled for a formal appearance before our corporate board of directors. My assignment was to present a summary of our operations and prospects for the region I was managing at that time, Central and South America. I carefully prepared and organized my presentation: I had my headliner. I had my middle and a good closer. All I lacked was a good opener.

For the opener, I decided I needed a bit of levity. I wanted the board to laugh. When I mentioned this to a veteran executive and experienced presenter in our company, he said quickly, "No! Forget it! This is a formal presentation." He reminded me, "You don't know the board members that well, and they don't know much about you. If your attempt at humor falls flat, you may do the same. Play it straight. Be totally businesslike. Be factual, be confident, be knowledgeable, be comfortable. That's what they want to see in an executive with your level of responsibility." It was good advice, and I followed it.

The second lesson for using humor is to be sure your material is truly funny. You may have noticed during TV talk-show interviews that professional stand-up comics frequently say "I'm always trying out bits of new material. I'll slip them in and try them on different audiences before I finally put them into my act."

Try out your humor in advance, with different groups of friends, in different settings and circumstances. Make certain people laugh before using it in some important situation. Don't take the risk of using material you haven't given several test runs. There is nothing worse than jokes that fall flat.

Other "don'ts" when using humor:

- Don't embarrass other people (unless it is a formal roast).
- Don't use ethnic or racial jokes.
- Don't use dialects.
- Don't make jokes about religion.
- Avoid any scatological or profane language.

Choose your speaking situations and your use of humor carefully. Know the situation and the audience. There are many occasions in business speaking where humor is totally inappropriate. Don't take risks. Try out your material in advance to assure it tickles the funny bone of the type of people who will be in your audience.

WHAT MAKES HUMOR HUMOROUS?

Humor stems from a few basic roots: the surprise ending, word play, physical actions (a la the pratfall), and topical humor such as current events or newsworthy people (Figure 12).

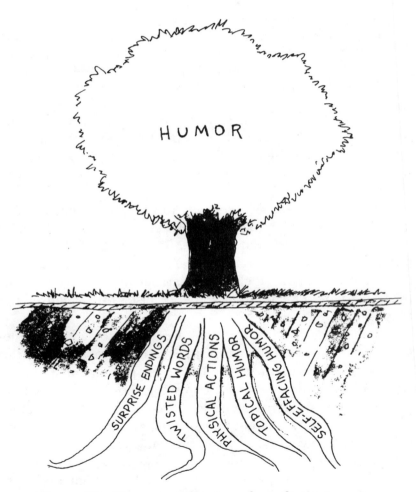

Figure 12 Humor usually stems from five categories.

A fifth technique is self-effacing humor. Here's an example of self-effacing humor:

> In 1989, football coach Lindy Infante of the Green Bay Packers was named the National Football League's "Coach of the Year." Shortly after, he told one audience that a news story about this honor appeared in his hometown newspaper with a misprint—instead of "NFL Coach of the Year," it said "NHL," which stands for "National Hockey League." Soon after the article appeared Infante received a letter from his high school football coach congratulating him on the honor. His coach wrote, "I'm glad to read you succeeded in hockey because I knew sure as hell you'd never succeed in football."

Some women in business, however, recommend avoiding the use of self-effacing humor because they contend businesswomen have enough difficulty gaining respect in the business world without tearing themselves down, even through humor.

True stories are another way to make speeches humorous. As I scanned hundreds of jokes supplied by comedy newsletters, I found that perhaps 98 percent of the entries just didn't sound or fit right *for me*. But among the remaining 2 percent, some special chord was struck and I was reminded of an incident in my life—or someone else's—that caused me to laugh.

And that's another tip: don't be afraid to "adapt" someone else's funny event to yourself. Stealing funny stories is an occupational entitlement used by even prominent, national speakers. The trouble with borrowing, however, is that no one enjoys hearing the same joke told over and over again. True stories, or true sounding stories, are fresher and more believable than canned or well-traveled jokes.

Dig deep into your memory and search for those true incidents that made you—or your friends, or family—laugh. Update those stories from the past, revise them. Try them on friends and listen carefully to what "works" and what doesn't.

Figure 13 Your daily newspaper can be a wonderful source of humor for speeches.

A third source of good, fresh and effective humor comes from daily newspapers or magazines (Figure 13). Here's a suggestion:

> Whenever you read something that makes you *laugh out loud,* clip it or write it down. Then, start relating it at cocktail parties or over coffee with friends. If it consistently gets a good laugh, put it in your file. Then, as you are preparing for some presentation, scan that collection to see if you can adapt and apply the story, even in loose fashion, to points you are making in your speaking situation. Avoid prefacing your humor with the trite phrase "I heard this joke . . ." Instead, weave your story into your presentation so the audience is almost unaware you are building up to a punch line . . . until you *punch* it.

Another good habit to assure that you use appropriate and appealing humor is, after your presentations, to keep written records on the stories that succeeded in particular situations. For example, certain humorous stories that are successful with business audiences sometimes fall flat with, say, groups of teenagers and, of course, vice versa.

A warning note. If you do manage to build something of a reputation as an entertaining and humorous speaker, make certain that the person who introduces you avoids saying, something like this, "This fellow is really very funny. I know you'll enjoy hearing him because he always gets his audiences rocking with laughter." Such testimonials raise the audience's expectations and usually result in disappointment that you are not equal to Jay Leno or Eddie Murphy or some other professional stand-up comedian. How do you avoid such an introduction? Sometimes it is not easy, since the presenter thinks of it as paying a compliment. However, you can politely ask the presenter what he or she intends saying, and even request the omission of any such well-intended comments.

"Timing is usually what separates professionals from the amateur," says Ron Dale, a professional comedian. "Some people never develop a sense of timing and therefore have difficulty telling a joke. Others—and this is a characteristic of many professional comedians—have literally been telling jokes all their lives. They were the class cutups in school, the practical jokers, the punsters, and the clowns. In essence, they have been practicing their timing all their lives."

Practice is the key. Dale says he knows one professional comic who even "rehearses his ad libs." And that's *not* a joke. That comic, according to Dale, has developed a repertoire of something like 120 ad libs that he has stored in memory. In this way the comedian can react quickly to hecklers or noises or other surprises that can and do occur when facing an audience night after night.

As a business speaker, you need not reach this level of professionalism, but you can learn valuable lessons from these more experienced experts. In essence, to develop good timing and good delivery of humor, just practice. That's all.

If you want to delve more deeply into the anatomy of humor in business situations, I recommend the book *A Funny Thing Happened on the Way to the Boardroom: Using Humor in Business Speaking,* by Michael Iapoce (John Wiley & Sons, New York, 1988).

SPECIFIC EXAMPLES

James C. Haney heads a 3,000-member association of manufacturers and commercial businesses. He tells about the time he spoke at a local retirement home. "When I finished," Haney relates, "I felt pretty good. I thought I'd done a pretty good job." After the program, a small, perky resident approached him and said: "Mr. Haney, my 8-year-old grandchild could have delivered a better speech than that!" And she turned and walked away. Haney was stunned. Soon after, some other residents came up to him and said "We just saw you talking with Clara. We thought we should tell you not to listen to anything she says. Clara just goes around repeating what she hears *other* people saying."

This is a true story, and when Haney relates it to audiences, it almost guarantees a good laugh. "It's an excellent example of a good 'opener,'" Haney explains, "because it is believable, it has that surprise ending that is so important, and it demonstrates that the speaker is unafraid to make fun of himself ."

In 1990, I was booked to appear on ABC-TV's "Good Morning America" show to talk about a recently released book of mine. Pleased and excited, I phoned my 94-year-old father in Colorado. "Dad," I said, "I've been booked on 'Good Morning America'!" He paused for a few seconds and then said "What's that?" After I appeared on the show, I called him and said "Well, how did I do?" Again, the pause. Then, with a

hint of surprise in his voice, he said, "Better than I expected."
I tried again. "Other than that, Dad, how did I look?" This
time he quickly replied: "Oh! You looked old."

This true incident—an example of self-effacing, true-life
humor—serves well as an opener. All you need do is follow
with a transition line such as, "So, today I hope I can do better
with you (the audience) than I did with my own father." Then,
launch into your topic.

Another effective trick used by experienced humorous
speechmakers is to string a series of punch lines together into
a chain. And, here the trick is to save the best line for last. For
example:

> The speaker's subject is the importance of clear communica-
> tions. To inject some levity into the topic of communications,
> the speaker reads certain excerpts from essays written by high
> school students that are decidedly *not* examples of good, clear
> communications. In these cases, the students muddled their
> history and syntax , resulting in mangled communication.
> The first student wrote about the Magna Carta. "What
> was the Magna Carta?" he wrote. "Well, it assured that no free
> man should be hanged twice for the same offense."
> The second student wrote about Queen Elizabeth I.
> "Who was Queen Elizabeth I? Well, she was known as 'The
> Virgin Queen.' When she exposed herself before her troops,
> they all shouted 'Hurrah!'"
> And, finally, this student was writing about the famous
> world explorer, Sir Francis Drake. "Who was Sir Francis
> Drake? Well, he circumcised the world. And he did it with a
> 100-foot clipper."

I've heard these lines delivered to different audiences a
dozen times and the reaction has always been the same: a
mild laugh after the first line about "being hanged twice for
the same offense." Then, a louder laugh over Queen Elizabeth's exposure and the resulting "Hurrah!" And, finally, an
even louder laugh over the malaprop "circumcised." But the

best laugh of all always comes after the tag line "And he did it with a 100-foot clipper."

Why is this? The answer is that the audience is pleasantly surprised at one successive punch line after another . . . and also that each line is slightly funnier than the preceding one. Proof is that whenever these three items were delivered in *reverse* order, the laughter did not build in the same way.

The lesson here is to string punch lines together, and then be certain to save the best for last. Also, we discussed earlier the importance of *timing* in humor. In the preceding example, it became important to *pause* for several beats between the line "Sir Francis Drake circumcised the world" and the final punch line: ". . . and he did it with a 100-foot clipper." Always let the chuckling or laughter subside before proceeding with the tag line. Otherwise, some people in the audience never hear the final words because they are still thinking and laughing about the play on the words "circumcised" and the intended word, "circumnavigated."

What should you do when a story or punch line falls flat? This happens even to the most experienced speaker. Minutes of silence seem to pass, but in reality it is usually only a matter of seconds. When this happens to you, move rapidly along and try to forget it. TV sports commentators tell us that one of Jack Nicklaus's many skills as a golfer is that after he has experienced a disastrous hole, he can quickly put it behind him and simply move on to the next hole. So it should be with speakers when expected reactions don't arrive. Just keep moving on.

Robert Orben, professional joke writer for several recent White House Presidents, advises that one way to "stack the deck" toward receiving that first hearty laugh is to observe the audience in advance and "spot someone who seems to be a good listener and an easy smiler and laugher." Then, establish good eye contact with that person as you relate your opening jokes. Having that person laugh not only stimulates others to laugh, but it serves as a wonderful confidence-builder for you, the speaker.

Quotations are another good device for producing smiles, with Yogi Berra being one of the most popular resources. ("When you come to a fork in the road, take it.") Numerous reference books filled with provocative and memorable quotations for the past several hundred years are readily available in bookstores and libraries. Refer to them when preparing your material. As indicated earlier, they provide the added benefit of provoking some forgotten statement or idea stored in the back of your mind.

Most of us enjoy hearing examples of double entendres, malapropisms, and mangled misstatements. Much humor is based on such misadventures with language. Author Richard Lederer has produced two wonderfully lighthearted books crammed with examples like these (including the earlier ones about the Magna Carta, Queen Elizabeth, and Sir Francis Drake). His first book was titled *Anguished English* (Laurel Press, Mill Valley, CA, 1987). This was followed by *Crazy English* (Pocket Books, New York, 1989). Both these books would be good investments for the resource shelf of any aspiring humorous speechmaker.

Another good resource book is Malcolm Kushner's *The Light Touch—How to Use Humor for Business Success* (Simon & Schuster, New York, 1990). Kushner provides the following five rules for successful delivery of humor:

1. *Learn Your Lines.* Practice the story and figure out which words to emphasize.

2. *Be Confident and Comfortable.* Don't tell an anecdote you are uncomfortable with. Enjoy the story yourself.

3. *Don't Announce That You're Going to Tell a Joke.* Sneak up on the audience. Surprise them with your funny line.

4. *Pause Just before the Punch Line, and Then Wait for the Laugh.* A one-beat pause just before the punch line adds emphasis to the key words. If you continue talking immediately after delivering the line, the audience will miss the impact.

5. *Keep It Brief.* An overly long anecdote or joke tends to bore an audience.

HUMOR TO BEND, BORROW, OR STEAL

The following collection of stories, quips, and anecdotes will jump start your own humor generator. As I discussed earlier, lists of jokes rarely seem to provide exactly the right humorous stories for you or your particular speaking situation. However, they are often useful to jog your memory, or you may be able to bend them to fit your speaking occasion. Of course, if you do find one or two here that tickle your sense of humor—take them.

(Ian Kerr, Public Relations counselor for Rolls Royce supplied this one.) "When I finished speaking at a large luncheon meeting, the emcee said that I had provided a 'Rolls Royce of a speech.' At first I was delighted, but then I realized that the two main characteristics of a Rolls Royce are that they are, first, inaudible, and second, they last forever."

When it comes to optimism, perhaps the best example I've ever seen comes from the surviving members of my father's high school graduation class. They still hold annual reunions, and each one has a special theme and slogan. For one reunion the slogan was "Help Me Make It Through the Night"; for another, it was "The Last Supper"; and the most recent one was "Stay Alive 'Til '95."

🖛 🖜

Just prior to delivering a speech, a division manager of a large corporation was nervously pacing in a room adjacent to the auditorium when a woman walked in. "Oh," she said, "You're our speaker today, aren't you?" When he nodded, she asked, "Do you ever get nervous before a speech?" "No," he said, "I never get nervous." "Then," inquired the woman, "what are you doing in the ladies room?"

🖛 🖜

(*A wedding toast*) This may shock some of you, but hear me out. I'm going to toast the bride and groom to *lie, cheat,* and *steal:*

> May they *lie* in each other's arms and comfort one another in times of anxiety and stress.
> May they *cheat* Father Time and live long and happy lives.
> And, finally, may they occasionally *steal* away to renew the love and affection they feel for one another on this very special day.

🖛 🖜

Rabbi Aaron Ilson offers this secret to assure that a speaker respects time limits. "Just before speaking, I put a lozenge in my mouth. I know it takes about 20 minutes to dissolve. When the lozenge is gone, I know it's time for me to finish my speaking. However, on one occasion I used this trick and when I looked at my watch I found I had been speaking for over 40 minutes. I then realized that when I reached in my pocket for the lozenge, I had mistakenly grabbed a loose button."

🖛 🖜

My wife and I were in the car listening to the radio. The guest on the talk show described a "Type A" person as one who is usually "successful, compulsive, above-average intelligence, high achiever, and neat." I commented that "I tend to be Type A, but I'm not compulsive." Wanting to agree with me, my wife said, "That's true. And you aren't above-average intelligence, either."

❦ ❦

(This one actually happened to me.) After I finished speaking, the emcee thanked me and, motioning to the audience, said: "This is the largest crowd we have ever had. And to all of you out there, thank you for coming. In fact, next time I hope you will bring a friend because our treasury could use the additional revenue. That way in the future we can bring you some *really good* programs."

❦ ❦

A friend of mine stepped up to the microphone, looked at the audience, and instead of saying, "It's nice to see so many old friends and familiar faces," said: "It's nice to see so many old faces and familiar friends."

❦ ❦

My first grader's teacher was telling Christmas stories when one of the children asked her to "tell that story about the guy who saw Santa Claus and got sick." At first the teacher was puzzled, but it turned out the child was referring to "'Twas the Night Before Christmas," where the father "flew to the window and threw up the sash."

❦ ❦

An American woman traveling in Southeast Asia was served bird's nest soup, a delicacy in that region. "Do you mean to say this actually is a bird's nest?" she protested. The chef assured her it was, explaining that the bird constructed the nest using its own saliva as glue. "Are you saying I'm supposed to eat saliva from a bird?" she said, aghast. When the chef asked what she would prefer instead, she replied, "I can't imagine anyone eating bird's saliva. Just fix me an omelette instead."

🖎 🖝

Whenever I fly on airplanes, I think about that famous "blackbox" that is so vital to find after a plane crash. I keep thinking why don't they make the whole airplane as indestructible as that black box . . . and secondly, when they ask what seat I prefer, I am always tempted to say "I'll sit wherever that black box is sitting."

🖎 🖝

I took my Latin American sales manager to Japan for his first visit there. When I introduced him to the Japanese delicacy of raw fish, called *sushi*, he poked at it and said, "What's this?" I explained what it was and that it was called *sushi*. He said, "In my country we call this bait."

🖎 🖝

Our language can be tricky. A college professor of mine wrote this phrase on the board: "Woman without her man is a savage." Then he asked the class to punctuate it correctly. The males wrote: "Woman, without her man, is a savage." But the females wrote it this way: "Woman! Without her, man is a savage."

🖎 🖝

When it comes to delivering the invocation at dinners, I'm *not* a good person to call upon. The last time I did it, I managed to screw up the silent prayer.

🖎 🖝

My wife always tried to teach our children good manners. One thing that bothered her was when our son would come home with friends and fail to introduce them to her. She always kept after him about proper introductions. Well, one day she was lounging in the bathtub when he burst through the bathroom door to introduce some of his new friends. I never had the nerve to ask her if she stood up to greet them.

Our local reference librarian reports that someone called and asked what the prefix "Dr." meant when a person was neither a medical doctor or dentist. "That probably means he is a PhD," the librarian explained. "It also means that person probably has a BS and a MS as well," the librarian added. "I know what BS is," the caller said, "so I suppose MS means more of the same and PhD means piled higher and deeper."

I was sitting at a conference one day when the speaker said rather emphatically, "The root of all mankind's problem is man, who is ignorant and apathetic." I turned to the fellow next to me and said "What do you think of that?" He replied "I don't know, and I really don't give a damn."

Working hard does pay certain dividends. We had a fellow in our office who took a briefcase full of work home every night. Later we found out he was stealing briefcases.

When I was in college, I was struggling to decide what profession to follow. So I took some aptitude tests. After they were evaluated, I received this letter: "We have examined all of your test results, your ACTs and SATs, your psychological profile analysis, and your vocational preference matrix. We have concluded that your best career and vocational opportunity lies in a field where your father holds an influential position."

(When receiving an award) I really don't deserve this . . . but then, again, I have arthritis and I don't deserve that either.

Most of the rest of the world uses the metric system. I suppose we in the United States will have to follow, but somehow it doesn't make sense to say "Give them 2.5 centimeters and they'll take 1.6 kilometers."

Here are some mangled metaphors uttered by politicians and taken directly from the public records of state legislatures:

- If it weren't for the Rural Electric Associations, we farmers would still be watching television by candlelight.
- I smell a rat and intend to nip it in the bud.
- This body is becoming entirely too laxative about some matters.
- These are not my figures I'm quoting. They're the figures of someone who knows what he's talking about.
- It's time to grab the bull by its tail and look it squarely in the eye.

Newspaperman Dan Satran reported recently that he sat through such a long introduction for a speaker he was tempted to whisper to the fellows at the table: "We have just listened to an introduction that needs no speaker."

While seated on the dais at a dinner one evening, the rather somber-looking man next to me said, "I notice you don't eat much before you speak. Why is that?" "Because," I replied, "a speech coach once told me, 'Full stomach means an empty head,' and so I don't eat." After I finished speaking and sat down, the man turned to me and said sourly, "You could have eaten the whole meal."

ROASTS

At least once in every business person's career there seems to be an assignment to help "roast" some honoree, whether it be for a milestone birthday or anniversary, a fund-raiser, or a retirement dinner.

Here are some ideas for zingers that you can adapt to your own special situation.

🖙 🖙

When I was asked to offer a few comments about our guest of honor, I decided this occasion called for some research. So I invited a couple of Tom's closest friends to go out for dinner so that we could compile a list of his accomplishments, his achievements, and his attributes. And *here (take two large folded pieces of paper from your pocket)* are the results. *(Pause.)* Two completely blank sheets of paper! It cost me $95 to find out this guy has had an absolutely colorless and uneventful life.

🖙 🖙

(It helps to find jibes that actually fit the character of the person being roasted. For example, if the person tends to be habitually late or slow moving . . .) "As you all know, time is not a top priority for Tom. He tends to be laid-back and unruffled. For example, he's the only person I know who takes an hour and a half to watch the TV program *60 Minutes.*"

🖙 🖙

He tried to be a chicken farmer once, but it didn't work . . . he planted them too deep.

🖙 🖙

He stepped in some cow manure one day and got terribly worried. He thought he was melting.

He wasn't too smart as a youngster in school. At his grade school spelling bee, he spelled "farm" E-I-E-I-O.

The IRS called him in for an income tax audit. They told him to bring his records, so he brought them two Frank Sinatras and a Barbara Streisand album.

He was asked to join the fight against malaria and he asked "Why? What have the malarians done now?"

Senator Robert Dole once opened a "roast" honoring White House political adviser Lyn Nofziger in this fashion: "I came here tonight prepared to talk about a man who has done a great deal for his country and his President. But since that meeting was canceled, let's talk about Lyn Nofziger." Later Dole added, "The President would have been here tonight, but he had a conflict. He didn't want to come."

INTRODUCTIONS

Finally, when it comes to *introductions,* for an unconventional and lighthearted introduction, here is one that I have used repeatedly with good results.

The objective is to depart from the standard and often boring introduction where a long list of biographical credentials and achievements are read, including college degrees and the names and ages of children. What follows rather immodestly provides my *own* biographical information, but it is provided to demonstrate how and where to substitute your own personal data.

Here is what I hand over to the person who has the assignment to introduce me:

Now it is my pleasure to introduce our speaker, Roger Axtell. On occasions like this, I find it helpful to do some research. Therefore, when I learned that Roger's 94-year-old father lived in Glenwood Springs, Colorado, I decided to write him asking for information about his son. Here is the reply I received:

Dear *(Insert introducer's name)*,

You wrote asking for information about my son, Roger. Well, how would you like to be:

- An advisor to three Wisconsin governors,
- A speaker in demand throughout the country,
- And, a tournament-ranked tennis player.

Well, so would Roger.

Instead, Roger worked 30 years for The Parker Pen Company until his retirement in 1986 as Vice President, Worldwide Marketing. He lived and traveled overseas for Parker for 25 years. This caused him to write four books: *Do's and Taboos of International Trade* is a "how to" book for business managers and is also used as a college textbook.

Do's and Taboos of Hosting International Visitors explains how to meet, greet, host, and entertain visitors to the United States. A third book titled *GESTURES: The Do's and Taboos of Body Language* describes over 200 gestures for 82 countries. And finally, *Do's and Taboos Around the World*, a general guide to international behavior, has sold over 150,000 copies in six languages.

All this has caused Roger to be interviewed on NBC's "Today" Show, the Merv Griffin Show, three times on ABC-TV's "Good Morning America Show," and dozens of other syndicated and regional TV shows. He was also once booked on the David Letterman Show but was bumped at the last moment by a dancing dog act.

He has, indeed, worked for three Wisconsin governors and currently serves Governor Tommy G. Thompson as his Special Assistant for Business. He does this for a dollar a year, which makes me wonder about his business sense and explains why I have his older brother handle all of my financial affairs.

I hope he does a good job at your meeting. He needs the experience. The first time he appeared before an audience was in the fourth grade when he portrayed Davy Crockett, and he wet his pants right on stage.

Signed: Albert E. Axtell

With that introduction from his own father, here is our speaker.

You, the reader, can easily adapt this introduction by changing the author of the letter to your own father, mother, husband, or wife, and by merely changing the biographical information. You can also insert your own true or slightly manufactured anecdotes. An introduction like this not only provides the audience with information about your background, but also cause the audience to greet you with smiles . . . always a delightful sight as you step up to the microphone.

6

Using Audio-Visual Equipment

We learn more by
seeing than by
hearing. Turn the
page to learn how
you can use this fact
to your advantage.

Actual Case Study: The president of an international shipping company is invited to one of the great American ports, Savannah, Georgia, to speak before a large conference on exporting. He views this as a wonderful opportunity to showcase his company and possibly win new customers: The room lights dim, and the executive begins reading from his professionally prepared script while using a remote control to flash a series of attractive slides on a large screen. Unfortunately, after the first dozen slides, the executive accidentally presses the "reverse" button instead of the "advance" button. The audience realizes his mistake, but he is completely unaware and continues reading and punching the wrong button. Finally . . . he looks up and realizes the picture on the screen has no relationship to his text. He fumbles with the remote control. Nervously, he presses the "focus" button, which just creates more confusion. He becomes flustered, tries to continue without the slides, but now cannot find his place in the script. Within seconds, his wonderful showcase opportunity disintegrates into confusion and embarrassment. The audience's unspoken conclusion is "How can you trust a shipping company that can't even operate a slide projector?"

This chapter will help you *avoid* just that type of nightmare in your business presentations.

The effectiveness of using audio-visual aids is well known:

- We learn 7% via hearing.
- We learn 87% by seeing.
- The remaining 6% is learned via taste, touch, and smell.

Audio-visual materials increase *retention of information*. People generally remember 20% of what they *hear*, 30% of what they *see*, and 50% of what they *both* hear and see. And if graphics increase comprehension and retention, they can also reduce meeting times.

Seeing is also believing. Graphics add credibility to presentations. Any time you put up a pie, bar, or line chart, or even a strong, declarative word slide, your message is visually reinforced.

Bear in mind that your audience has been nurtured on television, with all its clever graphics for advertising, sports, and news coverage. Contemporary audiences are visually oriented and accustomed to the best.

Another reason graphics are important is that more and more business gatherings have some members for whom English is a second language. For them, one picture is worth a thousand words, especially when those words may be glib American idioms, jargon, and buzz words.

The use of well-prepared visual materials also reflects on your image as a presenter. If your sales presentation, for example, follows one given by a competitor and your visuals are a cut above his or hers, the difference can only work in your favor.

In this chapter, you will learn how to select the right audio-visual medium for your purpose, plus the pros and cons for each type of visual aid. You will also learn something about how to design visual materials and how they are produced. A general briefing on equipment is also offered. Finally, I conclude with some general tricks and tips that will make you an audio-visual victor instead of a victim, like that poor fellow described in the case study that opened this chapter.

This chapter will *not*, however, turn you into a visual graphics technician or professional. It will, instead, equip you to work more closely and more smoothly with that increasingly important cadre of valuable technicians who, using the latest computer-aided devices, can produce dazzling slides, videotapes, and other sound-and-light shows. This new breed of specialists deserves your respect, and this chapter will help you learn how to work side by side with them in making your presentations shine.

Locating a top-notch but fairly priced production house takes a little research but the time and effort is definitely worth it—quality and cost can vary a great deal. A trade association, such as the Association for Multi-Image (AMI), would be a good place to start looking for a quality production house in your area. AMI is located at 8019 North Himes Avenue Suite 104, Tampa, FL 33614; the telephone number is 813-932-1692.

In the larger metropolitan areas," let your fingers do the walking" under such headings as "Slides," "Video," "Audio Visual," "Photography," and "Computer Graphics." You don't have to be a techno-wizard to talk with these people—just explain the nature of your talk, your audience, and so on. They will make suggestions and try to work within your budget.

Each agency may charge slightly differently, but most will detail the charge for each visual. Some houses bill according to the amount of time it takes to do the job. As in any business, you're usually better off getting a firm quote for the whole job than to leave it open for future interpretation by the agency.

WHICH MEDIUM FOR WHICH MEETING?

Once you understand that visuals can enhance your presentation in terms of interest, credibility, and image, your next step is to determine which medium is appropriate for your audience.

Here are some important considerations in choosing your medium:

- *The Purpose of Your Presentation.* You probably wouldn't want to have a videotape made for showing budget figures to your boss, any more than you would use a chalkboard to unveil a major new project before a large group of your peers in a convention hall. Neither fits the situation. (In the next section you will find a list of all the common methods for presenting visuals and the pros and cons for each.)

- *Audience Size.* The number of people in your audience will often influence what type of graphics to use. For example, the maximum size for a presentation using an overhead projector is somewhere around 100 people. A bigger audience requires a larger image, which generally cannot be provided with an overhead projector. Slides, or a canned video presentation, where appropriate, are the preferred mediums for larger groups.

- *Location of Audience.* What type of room will be used: A small conference room, or a huge ballroom at some hotel? Also, will you have to transport all your equipment and materials to some distant location?

  Or, must you rely on rented or borrowed equipment? Each of these factors may dictate the type of visual to be used.

- *Customs in Your Company or Industry.* What types of visuals are normally used by your peers and competitors? For small sales presentations, for example, flipcharts are often de rigueur. Consulting firms seem to favor high-quality slide shows, and advertising agencies often opt for multimedia presentations. There are, of course, exceptions to the rule, but be careful. If your organization encourages formal, documented presentations and you show up with handwritten overheads, your image and probably your effectiveness will suffer.

- *Capabilities.* The size of your budget, the length of time before your presentation, the availability of in-house equipment and expertise, and the need to repeat the presentation are vital factors in choosing the correct medium. How volatile is the information you need to present? For example, if the numbers are going to change at the last minute and you don't have a dedicated staff to produce slides quickly, then overhead transparencies might be the answer because they can be produced in minutes. The best rule of thumb is to choose the medium that can provide you with the most professional-looking visuals possible and still allow you adequate time to prepare.

WHICH AUDIO-VISUAL MEDIUM TO USE?

Following is a list of the customary choices among audio-visual methods, along with the pros and cons for each:

Chalkboard (or Whiteboard)

Pros	*Cons*
Best for casual presentations.	Slow, because you must produce words and graphs by hand.
Good when audience participation desired.	Little or no "glamour."
Inexpensive materials.	Presenter must work harder to keep audience interested.
No problems with equipment breakdowns.	Your handwriting may be difficult to read.
Mistakes can be instantly erased.	Ink markers can be messy and unreliable.
	Difficult to preserve and store results.

Flipcharts

Pros	*Cons*
Easy to produce.	Poor for large audiences.
Reusable.	Flipping pages can be slow and cumbersome, and pages tear easily.
Easily transportable.	
Inexpensive.	
Good audience participation.	Requires some artistic skill to produce each page.

Overhead Projection

Pros
Easy to use.
Transparencies made quickly and cheaply.
Colors and overlays can be used.
Room lights need not be dimmed.
Audience can see to take notes.
Allows on-screen editing and audience participation.
Computer-generated visuals produce stunning slides.
Other new technology allows display of 3-D figures and "live" computer data. (More on this later.)

Cons
Poor for large audiences (over 100 people).
Changing transparencies becomes distracting.
The speaker and projector can block view of the screen.
Light bulb can burn out in mid-presentation.

35-mm Slides

Pros
Better for larger, more formal presentations.
Visuals advance smoothly.
Photographic clarity and a quality image.
Slides are small, transportable, and durable.
Projectors readily available in distant locations.
Professionalism enhanced by using two or more projectors.

Cons
Slides can be expensive to produce.
Room must be darkened.
Inhibits note-taking and audience participation.
Operator can punch wrong activation buttons.
Slides can be inserted upside-down or become stuck.

Videotapes

Pros

Color, motion, and sound combine for top professionalism.

Best for explaining complicated subjects or processes.

Best for glamor and impact.

Best for extra-large audiences (via large-screen projection or multiple TV sets.)

Cons

Most expensive (e.g., $1,000 per minute to produce).

Shifts focus from presenter.

Projection equipment cumbersome and expensive.

Electronic Presentations

Pros

Visuals produced on a computer are sent electronically to a special projection unit for large-screen viewing. Therefore:

• Slides/transparencies/ overheads need not be produced.

• Projectors won't jam, bulbs won't burn out.

Easily produced fades, wipes, dissolves, and other effects.

Cons

Cost of projection equipment is high.

Trained technician usually required to advance visuals.

Clarity of visual not as good as 35-mm slides.

DESIGNING VISUAL AIDS

Choosing exactly the right medium for your presentation is important, and equally significant is the *design* of your visual materials. Here are some general rules for designing effective visuals:

1. *Write the Words First.* Develop your message, your headline, and your outline with its key points. Then consider which points in your outline need special emphasis. Graphics are to a speech what music is to lyrics; they enhance, complement, and reinforce one another.

2. *Use the KISS Method.* That is the acronym for *Keep It Short and Simple.* In other words, if possible, design no more than one main idea per visual.

3. *Use the KILL Method.* This comes from author and seminar leader Terry Smith, who recommends *Keep It Large and Legible.*

These two acronyms work well together because if you keep it simple, you'll usually have room on the visual to make your words and other graphics large, which is important.

4. *Use Descriptive Titles.* Titles on your visuals summarize whatever point you're trying to make. For example, the title "Sales Will Rise Sharply in 1993" is more memorable and meaningful than "1993 Sales." A good title can also help bring temporarily distracted audience members back into the presentation quickly.

5. *Decide on a Basic Design.* This means using the same colors throughout, the same type styles, the same cartoon character, or whatever it takes to show a continuing relationship between slides. Keep the design clean and standardize it.

6. *Proof, Proof, Proof!* Have someone else look over your work if necessary, but don't let incorrect data or a misspelling make you appear sloppy or ignorant. When you err, your audience gets the impression that you didn't care enough about your visuals to get them right, so why should they care enough to look at them?

7. *Allow Enough Time.* Give yourself ample time to prepare your visuals and to rehearse with them thoroughly.

8. *Use Visuals Sparingly.* If something can be stated simply, say it, don't show it. Flipping through a lot of miscellaneous visuals dilutes the impact of those that are important.

Even though you'll probably have someone else produce your graphics, it doesn't hurt to be acquainted with the various types of visuals commonly used in overhead and slide presentations.

Word slides or charts often flow very naturally from the script outline and can be incorporated into a presentation to "lead" the speaker through his or her talk. One method for organizing a presentation is to begin with a *title* chart with your name, the topic of your talk, and perhaps your company logo. The second visual could then list three or four main objectives or areas you plan to cover in your speech. Then, as you get to each area, bring up a slide similar to slide two, with the next topic highlighted.

Word slides are most effective as phrases, not complete sentences. *(Warning: Don't ever get caught reading your visuals verbatim or your audience will wonder why they need you up there at all.)* The words printed on each visual should be limited to five or six terse spoken phrases that complement the words on the screen.

One way of effectively using color involves what is called "progressive disclosure," or "build" slides. As you move down through a list of items in your presentation, each is highlighted on a new slide in white or optic yellow (against a dark background) and the previous items on the list are subdued in gray.

When using overhead projection, *overlays* can replace builds. Each piece of information is produced on a separate transparency and then laid on top of the previous one.

Overlays can also be helpful when disclosing progressive data on charts and graphs. They are most effective when produced on a computer so the alignment is correct.

Graphics are most effective when presenting complex ideas or data. But, a common question is "Which type of chart is best, or correct, for my information?" Here are some answers:

- *Line charts* show change of one or more variables over a period of time.
- *Bar charts* show the relationship between variables during specific time periods. They can also be used to compare parts of a whole with other, similar, examples such as profits versus sales from total revenues for particular years.
- *Pie charts* show the relationship between parts of a whole at one particular time.
- *Diagrams*, such as flow or organization charts, help the audience visualize certain relationships or processes.
- *Tables* show relational data in a precise form. They should only be used when the content can be limited to a very few cells, or blocks of information.

HOW VISUALS ARE PRODUCED

In recent years, advancements in the production of visuals for speaker support have been astonishing. For example, five years ago, the conventional method for creating graph and line charts for 35-mm slides involved physically cutting and pasting color panels, tape, and typewritten copy together on an artboard and then photographing it. It took hours of intensive hand labor.

Today, the graphic artist is much more likely to work with a computer linked to a variety of color output devices. These computerized programs can produce colored slides, overhead transparencies, handouts, and even electronic presentations.

So that you are familiar with the terminology and methods, let's now examine each of those visuals.

Overheads

When designed properly, handmade overheads can still look very professional. Try to avoid typewriter copy; instead, use text produced on a laser printer or by typesetting. (Either method will produce a variety of different type styles and sizes and is available at almost any print shop. Typesetters produce book-quality copy, eliminating the "jaggies" found in lower quality output.) Paste the copy on plain, white paper and, using a standard copying machine, convert the pages into 8½-inch by 11-inch transparencies. If the edges of your pasted-on paper create black lines on your transparencies, make a second paper copy of the original and use white-out to remove the lines. Then run it through as a transparency.

If you don't have access to a computer or a typesetter, there are lettering machines (Kroy makes a good one) that you can use to set type in thin strips for transfer onto paper. Most of these machines run less than $500.

Making the copy big and bold is all-important. Using all capital letters is normally a good idea. A good rule of thumb for testing readability is to stand 10 feet away from the transparency (when not projected).

Use cardboard frames for overhead transparencies. They provide the following advantages:

1. They keep your films from getting stuck together.
2. You can write notes to yourself on the borders.
3. They block spillover light from the projector.
4. You can number your transparencies in an upper corner for easy ordering.
5. You can tape overlays onto them easily.

Projection of Overhead Transparencies

Although many aspects of overhead projection have changed little over the years, there are a few new twists you might want to discuss with your audio-visual technician.

One of the technologies currently sweeping the overhead presentation market involves the use of a narrow, flat, box-shaped unit called a liquid crystal display (LCD) panel. This electronic device is placed on the viewing stage of an overhead projector where you would normally put a transparency.

When a personal computer is plugged into the LCD, visuals created on the computer (most commonly spreadsheets and other financial data) are projected in the same manner as a transparency. The presenter is saved the trouble of producing the physical film and the visuals can be generated just prior to, or even during the presentation.

Some of the other features now being incorporated into the newer, more portable overhead projectors include swing-down arms, lighter weight, and retractable cords. But if you're looking for one standard feature on an overhead projector that you simply cannot do without, the automatic lamp changer stands alone in terms of practicality. Anyone who has had to ad-lib in front of an audience while waiting for a white-hot bulb to cool can appreciate the value of automatic lamp changers.

Remember the old opaque projectors? Now they're making them so you can put color photos, circuit boards, blister pack merchandise, or virtually any small object in place of a transparency, project it on a screen, and discuss it at length while your audience views it on the big screen.

Quality overhead projectors start at around $300 and can run up to $15,000. Buhl Industries and Dukane Corporation make good workhorses for under $600. The 3M 2100 series represents a solid line, especially the 2150, which is remarkably quiet and, features a versatile lens system as well as an automatic lamp changer. It lists for around $900. (All prices are 1991 prices.)

Introduced in 1986 in monochrome (i.e., single-color) versions and priced at about $2,000, the newest LCD panels now boast more than 5,000 colors and can carry price tags of up to $6,000. You'll still pay between $1,200 and $2,000 for a quality black and white model. Sharp is a major player for either monochrome or color models, with Sayett providing one of many options for black and white.

35-mm Slides

The color slides you take during your vacation can now be produced by computers, complete with words and all kinds of other artwork. As a result, the old artboard method mentioned earlier has become obsolete.

Not only do these new computer-generated visuals look and communicate better, but the price for producing them, even through an outside agency, is reasonable. Word slides can be purchased for about $10, while graphs and charts may run $20 to $50 each.

The key to getting what you want out of computer programs is to know what kind of visuals you plan to create before you go shopping. All the popular presentation software programs will create word, bar, line, and pie charts, along with spreadsheets and a host of other visuals. Some are just better at certain applications than others. Aldus Persuasion, for example, is one of the easiest programs to use for creating word slides, organization charts, and other text-oriented visuals. If, on the other hand, you are an IBM PC user and most of the talks you give require the use of charts and graphs, you might consider Harvard Graphics a good choice. Users of Lotus 1-2-3 probably know that Lotus Freelance Plus does an excellent job of electronically converting spreadsheet data into visuals.

In general, it's becoming easier and easier to produce good 35mm slides. Programs are becoming easier to use, documentation is improving, classes are offered at computer centers and technical schools just about everywhere, and more powerful hardware and software are now available at very competitive prices.

The not-so-good news is that the initial cost of getting into electronically produced visuals can be prohibitive for many presenters. The software programs usually average between $400 and $700, but the hardware (computers, monitors, etc.) can easily run $2,000 to $3,000.

For those interested in creating their own visuals on a computer, I'd highly recommend *Making Successful Presentations, A Self-Teaching Guide,* by Terry C. Smith (Second Edition, John Wiley & Sons, New York, 1991). Smith includes an entire chapter on tips for purchasing a computer, the top software products currently available, and a host of other very useful information.

How are the visuals transformed from images on a computer screen to the actual, usable form, such as slides, overheads, and color charts? Creating these materials requires equipment known as "output devices," and as you may have suspected, this is where you can spend some real money.

The same devices are used for outputting both overhead transparencies and color hardcopy. The machines of choice are inkjet printers, color plotters, thermal transfer printers, and color laser printers. Here are explanations for each method:

- *Inkjet printers* produce usable color pages but fall short on quality when it comes to transparencies. It takes about 90 seconds to run a copy. Hewlett-Packard offers a popular model (the Paintjet XL), as do Canon, Sharp, and Tektronix.
- *Pen plotters* use up to eight different pens that move back and forth across the paper or transparency. Although they're slower than inkjet (up to 20 minutes per complicated plot) and the colors are limited, the output is generally very sharp. They also retail in the $2,000 to $3,000 range.
- *Thermal transfer printing* involves heating a plastic film that transfers wax onto a specially coated paper. The technology is improving, but the price still ranges from $5,000 to $18,000, depending on features. Popular manufacturers are QMS, CalComp, and Seiko.

The future of color printing, as with general office black-and-white printing, seems to be focused on laser technology. There are no truly affordable models out yet—a good color laser printer will run close to $30,000—but the quality is there. In the next few years, we'll undoubtedly see prices come down, as is currently the case with black-and-white printers.

Getting 35-mm slides produced involves electronically transferring computer-generated images to a film recorder, which exposes them onto photographic film (2–10 minutes per slide) for processing at a standard photo laboratory. Film recorders come in a wide variety of prices and capabilities, with the lower cost versions running from $5,000 to $10,000. Polaroid and Agfa-Matrix produce quality models in respective price ranges.

If the price and complexity of your output options have you a little deflated, never fear. There is an excellent alternative to investing thousands of dollars, and that is to use service agencies. For as little as $10 per slide or $6 per overhead, you can have the files you created converted to presentation format by these agencies. This is especially handy for slide making because even if you bite the bullet and purchase a recorder, the film must still be processed, cut, and mounted.

If the thought of purchasing a graphics software package or even a computer and associated output devices sounds appealing to you, perhaps it is time to ask yourself an important question: "Who should be producing my presentation materials?"

To answer this, there are several factors to consider:

1. How much time do you have to devote to it, and what is your time worth? Creating the visual is only part of the job. It has to be saved on a floppy or hard drive in an easily retrievable manner. If you're outputting in-house, your computer could be tied up for the entire 20 minutes it takes for each overhead to run through the color plotter.

2. If you need complicated diagrams, charts, and graphs made, do you have the graphics talent it takes to do the job properly? Within the industry, it's often said that you should hire graphics artists and teach them computer skills, not the other way around. For those interested in seeing what computer-generated material is all about before taking the financial plunge, service agencies are a good alternative. Prices can vary significantly—as can turnaround time—so it pays to shop around.

If, however, you're planning a simple operation and the costs are justified, creating your own graphics can be extremely rewarding, and you'll get exactly what you asked for every time.

Here is the minimum pricing (at 1992 prices):

- Personal computer, $2,000.
- Software, $500 to $700.
- Laser printer for black and white, $1,500.
- Film recorder for slides, $5,000.
- Color printer for overheads, $2,000.

Projection of Slides

For the past 20 years, the public speaker's best friend has probably been a 35-mm *slide projector.*

The Kodak Ektagraphic III line of projectors remains the industry standard, with prices ranging from about $300 to $600, depending on the options you choose. Some of those features are automatic focusing, high-intensity lamps, and wireless remote controls. If you plan to use just one multipurpose lens, the auto-zoom lens covers most requirements.

The traditional single projector at the back of the room with the screen at the front is no longer a presenter's only (or best) option. If you are not acquainted with *rear-screen projection,* the following explains how it works, along with the pros and cons of conventional versus rear-screen:

- A translucent screen is built into one wall, and the projection equipment, operator, and slides are positioned *behind* that wall, out of sight of the audience. In this manner, all the visuals are projected against that screen from the rear and the audience views the result from the other side of the screen.
- Rear-screen projection eliminates having a projector in the audience, with the noise of its cooling fan possibly disturbing members of the audience in that vicinity.
- Rear-screen projection also allows two or even more projectors to be used, which is difficult when those

projectors are in the back of a room, positioned amid the audience.

- Also, a conventional slide projector positioned at the back of a room casts a beam of light forward, and shadows from the heads of people sitting in the front center often interfere with the image. All this is eliminated with rear-screen projection.

- It allows you, the presenter, the freedom to move about in front of the visual image on the screen without casting a shadow. Also, pointers may be used more effectively, without casting shadows on the screen.

- Because of the high-intensity bulbs used with rear-screen projection, the room where the audience is seated need not be darkened as much as when the projector is actually in the room.

- The absence of projection equipment, operators, dimmed lights, and a strong beam of light all produce a classier setting.

- Finally, when two or more projectors are added to rear-screen projection, along with the technique of "dissolving" slides into one another, the result is a truly professional-level presentation.

Videotapes

With the explosion of home video cameras and VCRs, the current generation has become thoroughly familiar with the ease and joy and effectiveness of this form of audio-visual presentation.

Even an amateur to videotaping can grab a camera, go to a building site and return with a reasonably good visual report for all the people back at the office. However, when it comes to sales and training videotapes, or more sophisticated presentations, it's probably best to turn to professionals, and the best place to locate them is through the Yellow Pages of your phone directory.

Meanwhile, it might help for you to become acquainted with the most appropriate video *projection* equipment.

- *TV Monitor.* This is simply a standard television set (Figure 14). It is best for audiences of 15 or fewer people. A TV unit with a built-in video cassette recorder (VCR) is especially handy. Panasonic, NEC, and Sony manufacture a wide variety of reliable industrial monitors, ranging in size from 19 to 37 inches and in price from $300 to $3,000.

- *Portable LCD Large-Screen Projectors.* These price out at $3,000 to $5,000, but pictures are not yet top quality.

- *Cathode Ray Tube (CRT).* Provides excellent resolution but requires continuous fine-tuning by qualified technicians. They are priced between $5,000 and $50,000; two reliable manufacturers of data/video projection are Sony and Barco.

Figure 14 Single TV sets are best for small audiences.

A CHECKLIST FOR YOUR NEXT
AUDIO-VISUAL PRESENTATION

Now that your script is written, your visuals are ready, and you have rehearsed, here are some of the finer tips and tricks that will make your presentation look like a pro's:

- *Prepare to deal with bulbs burning out.* When using an overhead projector, check both the main lamp and your spare. For slides, get a spare projector. Then, if a bulb goes, it's much easier simply to replace the entire lamp assembly from the spare projector. Even though it only takes about five seconds, practice it to make certain you know how.

- *Avoid cardboard slide mounts on 35-mm slides.* They warp and get jammed in projectors easily. Plastic mounts are better, but the image may distort because the slides are not supported in the center. Glass mounts are best, but fully enclosing the film between two pieces of glass can allow moisture to create strange-looking whorls on the screen. Thus, single-side glass mounts are preferred.

- *Write the carousel slot number for each slide on the corresponding mount.* Don't use paper stick-on tickets because they could cause the slide to jam in the gate. Write the numbers in pencil in case you must change them. Once slides are marked, if you drop your full carousel of slides, you can at least reload them in order fairly quickly.

- *Always personally carry your slides or overhead transparencies onto the plane, train, or bus.* Luggage can be replaced if lost, rerouted, or stolen. Your visuals are more difficult to replace.

- *Practice removing jammed slides before your presentation.*

1. Check the slot number of the jammed slide.

2. Pinch the metal tabs (or turn the slot with a coin, depending on your carousel) in the center of the tray, and lift it from the projector.

3. Remove the jammed slide from the projector by pushing the SELECT lever next to the gate.

4. Make certain the slide ring is attached to the top of the carousel by turning firmly in a clockwise manner until a click is heard.

5. Turn the tray upside down and rotate the metal ring until the tabs fasten to the slot. Turn the tray right-side up.

6. Remove the top ring and replace the slide, if desired.

7. Set the carousel back on the projector, depress the SELECT switch and hold, while turning the carousel to the desired slot number.

8. Check the slide drop to make sure it doesn't jam again.

- *When using a videotape*, check with your projectionist well in advance to make certain the tape you have is the same format as the projector you plan to use.

- *If you will be projecting before a large audience*, view your tape well in advance before you decide to use it. If the quality is not excellent, large-screen projection will only accentuate shortcomings.

- *Use a laser pointer whenever possible*, certainly before a large audience. These pointers are small (some are about the size of a pen), can throw a small red dot of light over long distances (i.e., 50 to 100 feet), work in any lighting situation, and are easy to use. Laserex, Kodak, and Applied Laser Systems all sell consumer models for between $200 and $500.

Note: One caution about laser pointers. Use them sparingly during your presentation to prevent having the red dot begin to "bounce" on the screen because your hand or arm is not rock-solid steady. Rest your arm on the lectern to help keep the dot steady. When laser pointers were first introduced, technicians called them "nerv-o-meters" because the nervousness of the speaker could be gauged by how much the laser dot jumped around on the screen.

ROOM PREPARATION

The best way to determine if your facilities will be adequate for audio-visual presentations is to visit the room well in advance and ask yourself these questions:

- *Who is my main contact for facilities support?* Find one person responsible, and direct all questions and requests to that individual. This eliminates a lot of shoulder-shrugging and buck-passing. Also, meet the projectionist and sound technician to review every detail.
- *Will the proper equipment be available?* If not, bring your own.
- *Can I get the room dark enough to show my visuals effectively?* This is a job for your coordinator.
- *Where will the projectors be located?* Will they block my audience's view of the screen? Are they going to be positioned within the audience? Is there a possibility that equipment could accidentally get unpluged?

Note: If your electrical cord must trail along a carpet, tape it down with duct tape. If it must go under a sliding partition into another room, be sure you clearly mark the cord "Do Not

Unplug!" I know of two instances where hotel personnel unplugged projection equipment; in one case, they rolled up the extension cord and took it away.

- *Where will the screen be located?* For front projection, if at all possible, the screen should be positioned at an angle off to one side at the front.
- *What else could possibly go wrong?* Might background music unintentionally be piped into your meeting room? Are exit signs clearly marked in case of a power failure? Try to imagine what other mishaps might occur, and then prepare for or attempt to prevent them.

GENERAL TIPS

Once you've prepared the room by familiarizing yourself with the projection equipment and by checking the bulbs, extension cords, and remote controls, you're now ready to practice your talk.

Here are a few basic rules for using visual aids in any presentation:

1. *Face the audience.* When using a pointer, hold it in the hand closest to the screen so you can face them and maintain eye contact. Talk to the audience, not to the visual.
2. *Avoid reading the writing on your visuals.* Paraphrase them and then expand on the message the words convey.
3. *When using transparencies, shut off the projector occasionally.* This helps emphasize important points, and also gives the audience a bit of variety. One trick to avoid turning the projector light on and off is simply to tape a flap of paper over the projection lens and

flop it down over the lens when you want to darken the screen and direct the audience's attention back to you. Then, when you want to use the projection again, merely lift the paper flap up and rest it back on top of the lens.

4. If you must point to something on a transparency, use a pencil and not your finger.

SUMMARY

There you are—a new A-V specialist is born. With the proper preparation, proper equipment, and proper assistance, you'll have your audience giving you a standing ovation.

Here is a quick review of the major points in this chapter:

- Determine which visuals are right for your audience.
- Use the most professional-looking materials you can for any given situation.
- For best audience comprehension, keep the message simple.
- Proofread everything thoroughly.
- Let your visuals guide you through your talk.
- Finally, make sure you maintain that all-important eye contact so they remember *you*, and not just your graphics.

7

Appearing on Television

"You ought to be in pictures . . . and you probably will."

Prediction: The majority of businesspersons under the age of 50 reading this book will soon be appearing on television.

Why? How? When I told this to one young business executive, he smiled and said, "How can that happen? I'm an accountant. I can't imagine *ever* appearing on television."

The answer is found in one word: videoconferencing.

Regardless of your profession—accounting, engineering, manufacturing, marketing, or self-employed entrepreneur— the chances that you will appear on television during *any* business career over the next 20 years are close to 100 percent!

At this very moment, larger companies in the United States are installing and using in-house television studios for live videoconferences. They know it can be just as effective and less costly than full-scale meetings involving time-consuming cross-country travel with expensive air fares and overnight accommodations.

The phenomenon making this possible is the rapid expansion of a spiderweb of wires called fiber optic transmission lines across the United States. These tiny strands of microscopic light beams will make videoconferencing more feasible and economical. There is also discussion of creating franchised videoconferencing outlets across the country (a la photomats and convenience stores) to allow smaller businesses to buy videoconferencing transmission time.

It won't just stop there, however. The *second generation* of videoconferencing is already well past the experimental stage. It is called *3-dimensional imaging*. We first saw it popularized in the TV and motion picture series "Star Trek." So, by the year 2010, it's entirely possible that you, the business speaker (or at least your image), will be "beamed up" to a boardroom or convention hall in some distant city, in the same manner as Captain Kirk and his crew.

In essence, videoconferencing could become the facsimile machine of tomorrow as a standard means of business communications.

Even today, there is a thriving industry in videotape production for education and training, for marketing products, and for general communications from management.

Another challenge for businesspeople in this TV age is occurring daily as local and regional TV news teams increasingly turn to the business community for news and commentary. As a result, more and more of today's business managers find themselves standing before that electronic cyclops and appearing on the 5 or 6 o'clock news.

> *Case Study:* Media trainer Frederick Knapp tells of a senior officer from a top-ranked international company who agreed to appear on a Chicago TV talk show. He received some brief coaching on what color shirt to wear and what type of questions he might be asked. After one minute into the interview, the host started asking certain unexpected, penetrating questions. The executive first became ill at ease, then perspired heavily, and finally completely fumbled a critical question. Two actions resulted: First, after the president of the firm saw the tape, he immediately ordered media training for the entire top echelon of the company. And second, the senior officer was released a week after his TV appearance.

For the upcoming business executive of today, looking squarely into the eye of a TV camera and communicating smoothly and effectively will become a new and perhaps everyday challenge. The good news is that you can learn special techniques for appearing on TV so that you'll come across as a Tom Brokaw and not a Bart Simpson.

WHERE AND HOW TO START

Within the TV industry, the waiting room used by guests scheduled to appear on a TV show is called "The Green

Room." When I asked a TV producer how and why the sobriquet "Green Room" was adopted, he replied with a devilish grin: "Because so many people get sick there."

There are only two ways to prepare yourself for the stomach-testing experience of the "Green Room" and all the other unnerving surprises of TV appearances: first, through books like this one, and second, through professional training schools and seminars. There is no middle ground. You could practice in front of a home video camera, but nothing you do at home can duplicate suddenly walking into a blindingly lit TV studio or having a TV reporter push a camera and microphone into your face and start asking tough questions.

If you believe an appearance on TV is anywhere in your future, you will be well advised to read this chapter. *But while reading about it is helpful, a more thorough approach would be also to seek help and training through some type of professional workshop, seminar, or individual tutor.* With TV, it is important to replicate actually standing or sitting before a live camera being asked questions by a professional interviewer.

How do you find these specialized trainers and consultants? In large metropolitan cities, you can begin with the Yellow Pages of the telephone book. Look under the heading "Public Speaking Instruction" to find agencies and individuals who specialize in all types of public speaking. But, if it's TV interviews that interest you, look closer for those who offer special instruction in "media appearances."

If the Yellow Pages don't help, your contacts with advertising or public relations agencies can be another source of information. They probably know what type of training is available in your city or region; some may even provide classes on being "mediagenic." Also, local TV stations may know what training programs are available; some local TV personalities may moonlight by offering private tutoring.

The Chamber of Commerce of the United States (1615 H Street, NW, Washington, DC 20006, phone 202-463-5921) offers a variety of "Communicator Workshops" designed to "train business to meet today's communication challenge."

While these programs cover the full range of communication skills, several of the courses specialize in training and preparing businesspeople for both friendly and hostile TV interviews. "Communicator Workshops" tailor instruction to the needs of the individual or organization and are offered either at the Chamber headquarters in Washington, DC, or at the company site.

While there are many consultants and trainers across the country, here are profiles of just two services that specialize in television; they are representative of the types of training offered, fee schedules, and length of time required. (Chapter 10, "Resources for Help," provides more names and addresses of additional organizations that offer training in the full range of public speaking.)

MediaPrompt Inc. is located in Stamford, CT (phone 203-359-0728), and was formed by David Horwitz, former producer of "The CBS Evening News with Walter Cronkite." This firm specializes in training corporate executives to communicate more effectively on TV and radio, and in print interviews.

As an integral part of training, Horwitz sets up scenarios for his clients that simulate actual television situations including the physical and emotional elements involved. He tailors training to prepare executives for the following situations: TV appearances, public events, hearings, testimony, media crises, political campaigns, and videoconferences. He offers either private or small group classes and works extensively with videotapes so that the trainee can see how he or she appears on camera. The time requirement is a half to a full day. Fees run $2,500 to $4,000.

Frederick Knapp Associates, New York City (phone 1-800-321-2299) offers as many as 40 two-day seminars across the United States. These courses are intended to improve skills in business speaking, presentations, and image and style. They also teach participants how to do a better job with print, TV, or telephone interviews.

Knapp offers four types of seminars: "Execu-Speak" is a two-day seminar designed to develop and sharpen management speaking skills; "Execu-Style" is intended to increase a speaker's persuasiveness and ability to tailor presentations to different audiences; "Media-Speak" is a one-day program designed to polish skills in dealing with print, radio, telephone, and TV interviews; and "Execu-Image" is a two-day seminar on improving spoken communication, personal image, etiquette, and behavior, and choosing appropriate business attire.

Fees for the 1991–1992 period run from $595 to $895 per seminar.

Here are some of the TV problems and solutions you will experience in these workshops. Much of the advice presented here is excerpted, with permission, from a comprehensive instruction manual published by Horwitz/Mediaprompt for its clients.

NERVOUSNESS

Nervousness is natural. For most, appearing on TV is a totally new experience. The bright lights, the microphone, the unexpected quiet of the studio, the cool professional interviewers—it's like stepping on to a movie set. Suddenly, you realize "I'm on stage!" Your mind becomes numbed at the thought of the thousands of unseen people "out there" who are watching you.

Remember, the ways to reduce nervousness are to know your subject, believe in your subject, and practice. While it is difficult to practice for appearances on TV, you can *anticipate*, and the following sections describe some things you should know in advance that will definitely help reduce nervousness.

CLOTHING

If you feel comfortable about your attire and overall appearance, that will boost confidence and make you more at ease.

However, your choice of clothing should not detract the viewer's attention from your face and what you are saying.

Horwitz counsels that men should stick with grays, middle blues, and browns for suits and jackets. Women have more latitude but should stay with the middle tones. Watch out for reds. The TV camera often gives bright red a neon glow.

Also, both men and women should avoid plaids, herringbones, and checks. They tend to "vibrate and ripple on the TV screen," Horwitz explains.

Shirts and blouses should be lighter than surrounding jackets; pastels appear as off-white, which is fine. Stark white is usually avoided because it appears brighter than the face and eyes. That is why so many TV stations recommend that their guests wear pastels, and especially light blue.

Also, avoid shiny jewelry, such as earrings for women and tie clips for men. The lights cause distracting reflections.

MAKEUP

For on-the-spot TV news interviews, the time and situation factors usually prevent any opportunity for makeup. However, for in-studio interviews or for videotapes being produced for replay to business audiences, you should definitely consider makeup. The application of makeup is almost automatic if you are appearing on syndicated or national TV shows.

For men, the purpose is to eliminate the shine from oil and perspiration around the upper lip, nose, and forehead. It is also useful in hiding the shadow of a beard.

For women, your normal makeup base should be just fine, says Horwitz. Pay particular attention to your eyes. It is to your advantage to draw the viewer's attention to them. Eye shadows should be in the gray and brown shades; greens and blues tend to make a person look ghostly.

BODY LANGUAGE

Standing Posture

If you're standing at a lectern, make sure your shoulders are square to it. Avoid leaning on the lectern or putting your hands on it. Avoid shifting your weight from foot to foot because the camera operator will have to follow your weaving. To avoid such weaving, Horwitz says, place one foot slightly in front of the other.

Sitting Posture

This is the most common position for guest interviews and there are definite tricks to projecting a confident but relaxed image:

- Just before sitting down, men should reach around and tug their coattails downward and then try to sit on them. This eliminates any unsightly gap where the coat collar and neck meet, and gives a smooth, tailored look.
- Men should unbutton suit coats, lest the collars bulge upward when seated.
- Sit back into your seat, but lean forward enough so your feet are supporting a portion of the body weight. Keep your spine straight and forward, slightly away from the backrest, by leaning slightly forward from the hips toward the interviewer. "The result is a straight back, which makes you look vibrant, alert, concerned, and confident," Horwitz says. "Your clothes will hang better, you will appear to have lost a few pounds, and your body language says 'I care.'"
- Keep your chin up. Don't tuck it into the neck. When we tuck our chins inward, we tend to appear defensive.
- Plant your feet squarely on the floor with perhaps one foot slightly ahead of the other. That helps energize

your performance. For men, crossing the legs at the knees can signal defensiveness, and an ankle over the knee suggests overconfidence.

- For women, a natural crossing of the legs at the knees looks fine. Better yet, cross the legs at the ankles.

EYE CONTACT

A TV interview is basically a conversation. Everyone knows that eye-to-eye contact during conversations signals attentiveness, interest, and alertness. Therefore, focus your eyes on the interviewer's eyes in a friendly, considerate manner. But don't stare intently.

Horwitz counsels: "Break eye contact when you are gathering your thoughts, but go back to the interviewer's eyes right away. When gathering your thoughts, pick a spot other than the camera lens to look at. Also, try to avoid looking upward, lest you appear to be appealing to God for help!"

Some other don'ts about eye contact: Don't sneak a look at the studio monitor or the camera or lens, and don't let other people or movement in the studio distract your attention. The best and perhaps only time to direct your eyes at the camera is *when you are actually directing a comment to the viewing audience.*

There is an *exception* to each of these rules. It is when you are located in a remote studio being interviewed by a host at the main studio, as with Ted Koppel on "Nightline." In this case, there may be no other people in sight. You will be given an earplug to hear the program director and the interviewer. The camera will be pointed directly at you. In this case you should look and talk directly into the camera *just as though it were a person.* Again, it is often difficult to maintain a natural position. When the average person listens through an earphone, his or her eyes tend to look downward or to the side. Another temptation is to sneak a look at a monitor to see how you look on TV. Finally, it is a new experience to carry on a friendly, animated conversation with just a solitary, cold, round piece of glass staring at you.

GESTURES AND MANNERISMS

Horwitz warns that, for some unclear reason, the camera tends to *reduce body dynamics by about 30 percent* (Figure 15). He calls it "an energy drain." As a result, to avoid looking stiff and stilted while on TV, we must put more emphasis and motion into our faces and bodies.

One solution is to use gestures freely, but with these precautions:

- Be certain to keep them below the chin and at chest or shoulder height, otherwise the camera may miss them.
- Also, take care that your gestures do not cause your hands or arms to brush against the microphone that is usually pinned to a lapel or tie.

Figure 15   Television cameras drain 30% of the body's energy.

Try to use gestures that help the viewer visualize what you are talking about: sizes, numbers, directions, and so on.

Above all, don't be afraid to smile and laugh when appropriate. The smile is a contagious and universal language.

Horwitz schools his clients to *avoid* the following postural problems:

- If you are seated in a swivel chair, *don't swivel.*
- Don't cross your hands in front of your crotch. (That's called "The fig-leaf position.")
- Crossing the arms often appears as a defensive position. And putting them behind your back while standing suggests a military stance.
- Avoid playing with rings, pens, or pencils; rubbing your hands together; or tapping your finger on a table: You may distract the viewer.
- Other mannerisms that suggest you are ill at ease are chewing your lip, tugging at your earlobes, patting your hair, or tugging at a mustache. Professional actors can get away with some of these and look natural, but we amateurs usually cannot.

SELECTING YOUR WORDS

The typical TV news piece or interview with business types on the local 5 or 6 o'clock newscast rarely lasts more than two minutes. They may seem longer, but they aren't, says Virginia Sherwood, a former ABC correspondent who covered the White House and has since counseled businesspeople for the U.S. Chamber of Commerce. That means that—allowing for the "setup" time (i.e., the time it takes to introduce the subject to the viewer and to pose the question)—you, the interviewee, only have 15 or 20 seconds to reply. "And," Sherwood says, "you'll probably only have two of those 'bites' in which to provide your information and answers. If you ramble on and on, you'll be edited out." This is why the best, most effective TV interviewees can answer a question in a succinct 30 words or less.

In a studio interview session, however, more time is allowed. The typical interview is about four minutes. Once again, it is a virtue to keep replies short and to the point. Incidentally, there is no harm in pausing for a second or two before responding to a question. Such a pause is natural and gives the viewer the impression that you are quite properly taking a few beats to compose your reply.

As for additional general advice, Horwitz offers these tips:

- Think and speak for the ear. Short words are better than long words. Simple sentences are better than complex ones.
- Avoid jargon. Every business has its own lingo. Avoid using obscure terms or phrases that clutter communication and give the viewer the impression you are trying to parade your special knowledge.

ANSWERING HOSTILE QUESTIONS

Stereotypes aside, not every TV reporter is aggressive or crusading or trying to discover hidden secrets. They are simply trying to do a job, and they are trained to ask direct, incisive questions.

When confronted by what may seem "hostile" questions, your best reaction is, according to Sherwood, " to try to make a friend of the reporter. Respond patiently in a reasonable and even voice. Smile. Be honest and straightforward. If the reporter appears hostile, the audience will recognize this and quickly sympathize with your situation."

Here are more tips for dealing with TV reporters:

- Welcome reporters and their questions. Take the attitude that they represent the public, and that you want the public to know your side of the story.
- Don't ever argue with a reporter. Be positive. Stress the points you wish to make, even if you must repeat them several times.
- When a reporter asks several questions at a time, you might respond with "You've asked several questions. Let me try to respond to the main point . . . "
- Never evade a reporter's question with "No comment." That has become a pejorative phrase that causes the viewer to think "Oh-oh. Cover up!" It is better to say "I simply can't respond to that now for these reasons . . ." And then explain the reasons.
- Never lie to a reporter. It will surely come back to haunt you.
- Don't be afraid to ask a reporter to repeat or rephrase a question that you don't understand.
- If a reporter or interviewer asks a negative question (e.g., "Why have your sales dropped so drastically in recent months?"), try to avoid repeating the negative statement. Don't start by saying "Sales have dropped because . . ." Instead, start right out with the answer: "The recession has caused many of our customers to reduce inventories, but we believe this is only a temporary situation."
- Finally, never hesitate to say "I don't know the answer to that question" if that, indeed, is the truth. But then, try to explain *why* (e.g., beyond your area of expertise, all the facts have not been gathered yet, a final decision has not been made yet, etc.).

Above all, the best advice when preparing for a TV interview of *any* kind is as follows:

1. *Know* the subject. Do your homework. Make certain you know as much about the subject as anyone.

2. Consider one, two, or maybe three *basic points* that you wish to convey during the interview. Make certain you can relate them in brief, clear sentences. Keep steering the conversation around to those points. Don't be afraid to repeat your message(s) in different ways. Use examples and analogies that provide the viewer with mental images.

3. Try to *smile, relax,* and consider the experience as a conversation.

As Sherwood observes, "The object is to appear natural in a very unnatural situation. You want to be comfortable, in control, confident, open, and friendly. Reporters are short-term, instant experts who have simply taken some time to prepare a few direct questions. *You* are the expert. That is why you are being interviewed."

OTHER TYPES OF QUESTIONS

In Horwitz's courses, executives are tutored in all kinds of TV appearance situations. For example, he takes the *news conference* setting and breaks it down to its two basic components: the opening statement, and the question and answer session. He has his pupils practice maintaining good eye contact with the reporters, and not looking into the camera. "Deliver your answers to the reporters closest to the cameras," Horwitz advises, "because the viewer wants you looking in his or her general direction and not away at some remote spot."

In TV news conferences or interviews, there are *four* basic types of questions, and Horwitz drills his clients in identifying them and dealing with them. The four types are (1) information-seeking questions, (2) opinion and speculation-seeking questions, (3) off-target questions, and (4) hostile questions.

- "What is the future of your industry?" is an information-seeking question with a wide-open door of opportunity for you to respond.
- "Do you think your market share will improve this year?" is an opinion and speculation-seeking question and offers both risk and gain. If you avoid it, you appear timid and uncommunicative. But if you have something solid and positive to say, it is a ripe opportunity to communicate this.
- "If you were doing business in South Africa, would you be fighting for a policy of one-man-one-vote there?" is an off-target type question because it is hypothetical and asks "What if?"
- "Your company has never had a woman serve on your Board of Directors; isn't that reactionary and discriminatory?" is, obviously, a hostile question. The questioner is trying to stir up controversy by using an accusatory statement.

Through coaching and practice, businesspeople can learn to identify and cope with each of these types of questions. Professional tutors and trainers try to prepare their clients for every situation. Horwitz, for example, rehearses executives for everything from the "softball" interview to the "ambush" interview. Softball interviews deal with few hard or penetrating questions. "Informational" interviews will be friendly but more pointed and tougher. The videotaped interview may take 5, 10, or even 15 minutes; but the interviewer may only intend using 15 or 30 seconds for insertion into a longer story. In an "on-the-fly" interview, a reporter and camera person suddenly confront you with a question such as "There's been a big explosion at your factory. What can you tell us about it?"

Any viewer of CBS's "60 Minutes" TV program has seen what Horwitz calls the "investigative interview" or the "ambush interview." A reporter on such an investigative assignment can represent a potential problem for you and your company. "Don't ever agree to an interview unless you know what it's about," says Horwitz. "And don't lie or bluff your way through such an interview." In the "ambush" situation, the reporter leads you through a series of innocent-sounding questions and then pops up with the surprise question, such as "Well, I have here an internal report from November 1991 that says your own people recognized this problem and nothing was being done about it." In this case, your answer depends on whether or not you are familiar with the document, but the proper reaction is to remain unflustered; do not look guilty or express anger.

IN-HOUSE VIDEO PRESENTATIONS

On occasion, you may need to videotape a presentation for purposes of training, education, or general communications. In this case, Horwitz tells his pupils, "This is the time to look the camera directly in the eye. That is because you want to deliver a direct, personal message, usually to small groups watching you on a normal-size TV screen."

This same advice applies when involved in videoconferencing. Try to treat the camera as "another person."

Bear in mind that the beauty of videotaping is that you can rehearse your presentation, deliver it many times, and then edit out mistakes and retain the best versions.

The essential qualities in these situations are energy, confidence, command of your material, sincerity, and friendliness.

Horwitz defines each of these as follows:

- *Energy* means a sparkle in the eye, an electricity in the voice, and a sense of enthusiasm and excitement. It does *not* mean phony drama or exaggerated gestures.
- *Confidence* comes from knowing your material and also realizing that the camera is especially adept at detecting both confidence or the lack of it.
- *Command of your material* means knowing all the facts, having statistics, citing examples, and using analogies.
- *Sincerity and friendliness* are obviously winning elements of public speaking, and the best way to exhibit them is to treat the interviewer and the viewer as friends.

SUMMARY

If you are invited to appear on television, whether it be for a brief on-the-spot news interview or for a longer session at a studio, Horwitz and Sherwood offer the following tips on how to prepare and anticipate:

- Have associates help you prepare a list of questions the interviewers could ask. Consider even the worst possible questions.
- Make certain you have all the information available— statistics, references, sources, examples—to answer these questions.
- Have your spouse or associates help you with "dry runs." The more you practice your answers, the more confident you will become and therefore more effective as well.

- If time permits, videotape these rehearsal sessions to observe if you are using good eye contact, good posture, and not unconsciously using distracting motions.

- If it's a studio interview, watch the program in advance so that you are familiar with the setting and the format of the show.

- When time permits, carefully consider what clothing you will wear.

- Arrive at the studio early, and if possible, meet the people who will be interviewing you.

- Above all, try to adopt an attitude that "this is just a friendly conversation" and "the only ingredient I might add is to show a bit more energy in my words, my face, my gestures, and all my reactions."

And don't forget to smile!

Special Speaking Situations

How to Introduce
Other Speakers

Serving as an Emcee
or Moderator

The Question and
Answer Period

Speaking to
International
Audiences

HOW TO INTRODUCE OTHER SPEAKERS

When David Ryan was asked to introduce the seminar speaker, he stepped up to the lectern and the nightmare of all speakers greeted him: His mind went blank—he could not remember the name of the speaker. Thinking quickly, however, Ryan said to the audience: "Before we begin, I just want to check out in the hallway to see if any more people are going to join us." He then stepped outside, glanced at the notice board where the speaker's name was printed, and returned to fulfill his assignment.

Serving as an "introducer," or "presenter," is a task that seems to befall just about everyone at least once in a business lifetime. On the surface, it appears to be such a simple assignment: Just give the person's name and recite the standard biographical facts.

Next time you're tapped for that job, however, push that personal history handout aside. You can do the audience, yourself and the speaker a big favor by using the following common-sense guidelines.

1. Keep it short. Two minutes, maximum. Shorter if possible. (Most people speak at a rate of about 110 words per minute, so you can use that as a measuring stick.) I was once introduced by a senior member of a state-wide association who started reminiscing about the association and wound up talking for 30 minutes!

2. You'll probably have to read the introduction, so write it out in large type on 5- by 7-inch cards. However, here's the secret: Within a reasonably short time before you step up to the lectern, find a deserted room

and read the material aloud at least six times. This practice session will make you so familiar with the information that you will be able to look up from the notes frequently to gain that all-important audience eye contact discussed in Chapter 4.

3. Remember that your job is to aid the audience by providing them with answers to three of the Six Magic Questions presented in Chapter 2. In this case, those questions are:

- *Why* this subject is timely for this particular audience.
- *Who* this speaker is.
- *What* credentials this speaker brings to this subject.

4. To serve the speaker, your role is to get the audience *eager* to hear him or her. Again, that's why the first point on this checklist—make it short—is so important.

5. To help yourself, and to make a good impression on the audience, you want to appear smooth, friendly, and capable. You achieve this by spending time preparing,and then practicing the introduction, even though it may last only a couple of minutes.

Next, here is a sequence of steps to help you accomplish all these guidelines:

1. Several days or even weeks before the event, contact the person you are introducing to discuss your introduction. This assures accuracy and appropriateness. It also avoids the problem of having to make last-second changes on the day of the program.

2. On the day of the event, before the audience assembles, be certain personally to check the microphone, the lectern, and where you and the main speaker(s) will be seated.

3. If you have not met the speaker in person before, introduce yourself to him or her long before stepping up to the dais.

4. Determine with the program managers if there should be a question-and-answer period. If so, follow these rules:

   • Be certain to mention this in your introduction.

   • Decide, with the program manager, how much time should be allowed.

   • After the speaker has finished, rise to lead the applause and remind the audience that the speaker has graciously agreed to answer questions.

   • To prime the question process in the event of that embarrassing and almost inevitable silence, have one or two questions of your own to ask the speaker.

   • Help the speaker remember to *repeat* the question so that everyone in the audience knows it. If the speaker forgets, step up to the microphone and do it yourself.

   • A few moments before the allotted time runs out, advise the audience that there is time for the speaker to answer "just one or two more questions."

   • At the end of the last answer, thank the speaker and once again lead the applause.

If there is no question-and-answer period, it is usually the assignment of the presenter not only to thank the speaker but to offer a few summary comments. These remarks should be brief (about 30 seconds) and should capsulize some of the key points made by the speaker.

To do an introduction par excellence, you might consider telephoning or writing close friends of the speaker to ask for phrases or anecdotes that help describe the unique credentials of the speaker. Only one or two choice phrases or brief stories are needed. This technique also conveys the message to both the audience and the speaker that you considered your assignment conscientiously and put extra work into it.

One of the cleverest introductions I've heard was given by the president of a large utility company for the mayor of his city. He simply said: "And now it is my great pleasure to introduce the mayor of our great city, John Norquist." Then, at the conclusion of the mayor's remarks, the presenter offered this pleasant and surprising closer:

> Thank you, Mr. Mayor. Now, you may have wondered, sir, about the relatively short introduction I gave you preceding your remarks. The reason for that was that there is an unwritten rule of protocol that says the more famous the speaker, the shorter the introduction. For example, if I had the honor of introducing God to this audience, all I would need to say is "Here's God." Therefore, your introduction had to be a little longer than that . . . but not much.

SERVING AS AN EMCEE OR MODERATOR

This job has been likened to being a gatekeeper at a bullfight. Your responsibility is to open and close the gates to let the bull enter.

A "gatekeeper" is a proper analogy. You are not the star or even the featured player. Instead, you are the facilitator, the timekeeper, and bridgemaker all rolled into one.

Once again, here is a checklist to consider next time you are tapped to be the master of ceremonies, emcee, moderator, toastmaster, or whatever term you prefer:

1. Meet with the program planners days or even weeks in advance. Develop a clear understanding of the goals of the meeting, the type of program desired, and the specific nature of the audience.

2. Lay out a specific timetable with the planners. If you plan on several 10-minute presentations, allow 12 or even 15 minutes for each. The reason is that very few speakers are disciplined to speak within given time limits.

3. The customary role of the emcee is to offer a welcome and then simply introduce a series of speakers in some prearranged order. Learn from the meeting organizers if more than that is expected of you, such as also giving the invocation, recognizing dignitaries in the audience, or making other special announcements. When introducing a head table, always ask the audience to refrain from applauding until the last person has been introduced. The only exception to this might be if you have a number of important luminaries seated at the head table who individually *deserve* the audience's applause.

4. Prepare notes about the people you are introducing, following the guidelines offered earlier. Above all, check on the proper *pronunciation* of each speaker's name. If it is an unusual name, be sure to practice saying it aloud because it reflects badly on you, as the emcee, to stumble over the name of a featured speaker.

5. On the day of the event, before the audience assembles, be sure to do the following:

   • Check out the room, the podium, the lectern, and the microphone. This is for your own comfort and familiarity but also to assure that everything is in proper working order.

   • Introduce yourself to each participant. Confirm where each person is expected to sit and the order of appearance (unless the program manager takes this responsibility.) The emcee should sit as close to the microphone as possible to avoid delays between presentations.

- If the microphone must be adjusted according to the different heights of the various speakers, try to anticipate this in advance. A good emcee will, as a courtesy, raise or lower the microphone to suit the next speaker as he or she approaches the lectern.

- Once you've made the introduction, remain standing until the speaker is positioned to speak. Then sit down.

- Determine with the program planners if there will be a question-and-answer session, and then advise the audience early in the program.

- Learn who will be responsible for monitoring the volume of the sound system, the room lights, and any other audio-visual equipment. Review, in advance, any special requirements with them and if and how you will cue them.

- Be certain to carry your notes with you and remove them each time you step up to the lectern; or place them on a shelf under the lectern.

- Most important, learn from the program organizers how long the program is expected to last. Try to begin on time and then try to finish at the desired time. The mark of a good emcee is to run a program on time.

- Finally, keep reminding yourself that your role is to keep the program moving along briskly yet smoothly. It is also useful if you have prepared in advance a final observation or thought or quotation that captures the essence of the meeting. Your words will be the final words the audience hears. They will be the words the audience remembers best as they file out of the room.

Professional emcees will also have assembled a collection of possible but appropriate one-liners or short anecdotes to insert between appearances of the speakers. The more experienced emcees will be able to fashion these from the direct remarks of each speaker, but that is difficult and sometimes dangerous to attempt. An emcee must never, never accidentally embarrass any of the speakers on the program.

Finally, an anecdote that demonstrates how *not* to be a smooth, diplomatic emcee:

> Alan Fredericks, associate publisher of *Travel Weekly* magazine, while visiting the People's Republic of China, attended a large banquet given by his Chinese hosts. At the end of the evening, the English-speaking Chinese emcee rose, raised his glass of wine and said: "A final toast. Thank you all for coming. Now, go home."

THE QUESTION-AND-ANSWER PERIOD

One of the more difficult assignments for an emcee is managing the question-and-answer period. Most of them seem to begin with these words from the emcee: "And how our guest has agreed to answer some of your questions." Then . . . silence. And more . . . silence.

Crowd psychologists attribute this to a simple but understandable phenomenon that "No one in a crowd likes to be first. A crowd longs for a leader." Here are a few tricks to overcome that embarrassing pause. If hands do not shoot up immediately, you can do one or more of the following:

- Offer the first question.
- If the speaker does not see any hands raised, he or she can then step up and say, "One of the most common questions asked me by audiences is . . ."

- The safest technique of all is for the speaker to "plant" a few questions with members of the audience. This can be done diplomatically if someone poses an interesting question *before* the speech, perhaps during informal conversation. In that case, the speaker or emcee can just say, "That's a very good question. I hope you'll ask it during the question-and-answer period."

- Another method is to arrange to have questions written out by the audience in advance. This is especially appropriate if you believe some members of the audience would feel awkward asking a question in public.

All these techniques have the same objective: to assist people in the audience so that the questions begin to flow. Bear in mind that people usually ask questions for one of three motives:

1. The questioner sincerely seeks more information.
2. The questioner is less interested in the answer but wants to show off his or her own knowledge. These questions are usually long and involved. One way for the speaker to cope with this situation is to say "So, your question is . . ." and then paraphrase and shorten it, answer it, and move on to the next raised hand.
3. The hostile questioner is someone who strongly disagrees or wishes to embarrass the speaker. In this case, the speaker should be cool, factual, friendly, and brief.

After a member of the audience asks a question, unless it is absolutely certain that everyone in the audience heard the question, the speaker (or, if necessary, the emcee) should quickly repeat the question over the microphone.

When, as speaker, you are answering, remember "Less is more." Try to keep from wandering. Try to answer clearly and succinctly. You can even pause for a few beats before answering, to collect your thoughts. Audiences will understand. It's very natural to pause and contemplate for a few seconds.

Also, when answering, try to steer your comments back to your basic message.

If you realize your answer must necessarily be complex or apply only to a small portion of your audience, just say "That's an interesting question but involves a complex answer. I'll be glad to meet with you at the close of this program to discuss it further."

If you honestly don't feel qualified or capable of answering the question, don't be afraid to say so. As the saying goes, "Better to be silent and be thought a fool than to keep talking and prove it." Do try, however, to explain *why* you are unable to answer.

Try not to become defensive, and never embarrass anyone in the audience. If you suspect someone is being hostile or purposely disruptive, try to counter with friendliness and kindness.

Either the speaker or the emcee should be assigned the responsibility of watching the clock to determine when the question-and-answer session should end. The designated person then simply announces, "We have time for just one or two more questions."

Try to end on a high note—that means, when you believe you've given a good answer or when the audience interest level is still high. Reason: It's an old show business axiom to "leave your audience wanting more."

The skilled speaker will also have a "closer" prepared to wind up the question-and-answer session. Here are two examples:

I've noticed our program chairperson looking at his (or her) watch, so I guess we should end this session. Will Rogers was asked once if it bothered him when people in his audiences looked at their watches. He replied, "No. The only time it bothers me is when they shake their wrists and put the watch up to their ear to see if it's still working."

☙ ❧

I appreciate and thank you for your questions. In closing, perhaps you read in the papers about the archbishop from Italy who recently visited the United States. It was his very first visit, and so his aides warned about the American media and how they often asked tough, even embarrassing questions. When the archbishop held his press conference at the airport, sure enough, one of the reporters asked, "How do you like the looks of American women?" The archbishop, realizing this was one of those dangerous questions, simply said, "Oh? I've just arrived. Are there any women in America?" And everyone laughed. The next day one newspaper featured a photo of the archbishop with the caption: "Archbishop's first question on arrival at airport is 'Are there any women in America?'"

SPEAKING TO INTERNATIONAL AUDIENCES

In 1991, a record number of international visitors came to the United States—more than 40 million of them. Many came as tourists, of course, but an increasing number of those visitors came to attend business meetings, conventions, and trade shows here. Further, an equally heavy flow of Americans head toward overseas locations each year, many for the same reasons.

As a result, more and more of our business audiences have an international flavor so it's important to consider some precautions. Here are some tips to ensure that you, as a speaker before one of these worldly audiences, don't trip over some cultural boundary lines.

1. First, Americans are lucky; English is the language of business throughout the world. Furthermore, English is commonly taught in schools around the world. In

Russia, for example, there are more *teachers* of English than there are *people* in the United States who speak Russian. And in the People's Republic of China, there are more people *studying* English than there are people in the whole United States.

2. The key point, however, is that Americans should remember that all those foreigners may not be learning *American*-English. And, if they have, in fact, learned English-English there can be hundreds of words and phrases that mean something entirely different from American-English. As just one example, England and the United States use different words for no less than 60 components when designating the various parts of an automobile between England and the United States (e.g., our muffler is called a "silencer" there, our windshield is the "windscreen," and the dashboard is the "fascia").

3. As a result, it is essential when speaking to an international audience to do the following:

   • Avoid colloquialisms, slang, jargon, buzz words, acronyms, and sports and military terminology.

   • Speak slowly, with a deliberate pace, yet don't become monotone or lifeless.

   • Use examples and stories. Repeat major points. And use plenty of graphics. One excellent technique is to make a point, then tell a story that illustrates that point.

4. If you must use technical terms, stop to offer brief definitions.

Rudy Wright, a certified meeting planner in Denver, specializes in helping clients stage meetings overseas before international audiences. Wright offers this additional advice:

- When giving a technical talk, provide a printed abstract or outline to each member of the audience.

- Respect the protocol of the local country. In other words, inquire in advance about the proper local courtesies (e.g., recognizing dignitaries in the audience, proper use of names and titles).

- Since most of the rest of the world uses the metric system, consider if you should either convert all your measurements to metric or supply them in both systems.

Humor becomes especially difficult when speaking to international audiences. American humor is usually topical or based on word play. Both of these are difficult to export and translate. Consequently, test your humor in advance with locals to make certain it will be considered funny.

Finally, there is the totally new experience in public speaking of using a foreign language interpreter. In some rare cases, where the complex facilities are available, you may have the luxury of *simultaneous interpretation*. More likely, however, you will use a *consecutive interpreter*. In the latter case, consider these special conditions:

1. When speaking through a consecutive interpreter, it is customary for you, the speaker, to voice a sentence or two constituting a single point or thought, and then the interpreter converts that into the local language. This continues, back and forth, throughout your presentation. Two points are critical to remember: Your speech will take *twice* as long, and you should deliver the message in short, compact phrases and sentences.

2. Spend time in advance with your interpreter so that he or she becomes acquainted with your voice, vocabulary, pace, and especially your special phraseology.

If you don't, you could run the risk of suddenly seeing some startled looks. It even happens to U.S. Presidents:

> When former President Jimmy Carter visited Poland in 1977, his interpreter was new and apparently unaccustomed to Carter's choice of words. First, when attempting to say Carter had "left the United states that day," he said Carter had "abandoned" the United States. Next, he translated Carter's phrase about the Poles' "desires for the future" as their "lusts for the future." And, finally, he pulled the biggest whopper of them all by saying "The President says he is pleased to be here in Poland grasping your secret parts."

3. Arrange for a separate microphone for the interpreter. This saves the problem of the two of you bobbing back and forth, sharing the same mike.

4. Speak to the audience, not to the interpreter. Don't lose that valuable eye contact with your audience.

5. Don't be afraid to show emotion in your language, even though some or all of the audience may not understand your words. It is still important to transmit energy, strength, and conviction, and you can do that with your voice and your body language.

6. Take time to rehearse with your interpreter, so that you become comfortable with each other. This helps you smooth out bumpy spots, become acquainted with the back-and-forth pace, and encourages short but complete sentences.

7. Agree with your interpreter on prearranged signals, so he or she can indicate if you are going too fast or too slow.

8. Memorize at least a few polite phrases in the local language so that you can begin and end your speech on a gracious note. For example, "Thank you for your patience in listening to me," or "You have been a very gracious audience; thank you." This attempt at speaking the local language usually ingratiates the speaker to the audience.

9. Find some way to thank your interpreter, either publicly or privately. Also, after your speech, evaluate the results with the interpreter so you can be even smoother the next time around.

Speaking to international audiences can produce memorable moments. I once entertained a distinguished business visitor from Bogotá, Colombia. At the banquet in his honor, he asked me if it would be appropriate if he offered a toast. He said it was an old Spanish toast that he would attempt to translate into English. I assured him it would be fine, and this is what he said in his halting English:

Ladies and gentlemen. I am so very pleased to be in attendance here this evening. Let me propose this special toast from my country. This is absolutely the most enjoyment I have *ever* had . . . dressed.

While there was a momentary silence from the audience, they quickly grasped the situation and not only applauded but gave our guest a standing ovation.

How to
Turn Professional

"To graduate from a 'wannabe' to a 'willbe' status, it's important to make the climb carefully, step by step."

This chapter details how to prepare and then get launched as a professional. As you will soon learn, it usually takes considerable preparation, patience, and perseverance before you can ascend to the professional dais.

But the rewards can be worth the climb. Speaking professionally can become a full-time occupation, or complement a bustling career, or serve as a wonderful retirement avocation. Whichever is your objective, it can also be challenging, invigorating, and ego boosting.

HOW TO START

The first requirement is to have a *specialty*. In marketing terms, the word is "positioning." That means you must carve out a position within the marketplace that is unique and appealing when compared with other professional speakers around the country. Two good examples of people who in 1991 became immediately "positioned" and appealing as professional speakers were U.S. Army General Norman Schwarzkopf of "Desert Storm" fame and Dave Dravecky, the baseball pitcher whose pitching arm was amputated after a courageous battle with cancer. Schwarzkopf started at the highest rung of the ladder, incidentally, being offered as much as $80,000 for a single speech. Now that's positioning!

One common mistake would-be speakers sometimes make when starting out is to attempt to be all things to all audiences, by claiming they can speak on any number of topics. That usually fails. You *must* have a specialty, whether it is as an athlete, educator, successful business entrepreneur, politician, humorist, or expert on some specific topic of wide, general interest.

One category in high demand is the inspirational/motivational speaker. Lou Holtz, the Notre Dame football coach, is one of the most successful of these. In Holtz's case he has immediate "positioning" credentials as a successful, nationally known football coach. But he is also a compelling platform speaker on leadership, planning, goal setting, teamwork, and perseverance. He even uses his ability as an amateur magician to spice up his talks.

Lee Sherman Dreyfus is a former college president, president of an international insurance company, and Governor of the State of Wisconsin. He is now a full-time professional speaker, delivering about 80 speeches a year. While he tailors each one, depending on the nature of the audience, his basic messages deal with education, the American way of life, and the opportunity for the future. More often than not, Dreyfus receives a standing ovation.This ability to motivate people has been cultivated through decades of experience speaking in lecture halls, corporate board rooms, and on the campaign trail. Is he enjoying this new life? Absolutely, and that fact is underscored in his personal slogan: "Have mouth, will travel."

The most popular specialties break down into two categories: Topics that appeal to individuals, which are usually best presented in seminars and workshops, and topics that appeal to groups, which are best presented at luncheons and banquets. For individual appeal, specialties in constant demand are such things as how to sell better, how to communicate more effectively, how to relieve stress and anxiety, how to organize your life more efficiently, how to think and act positively, and how to live a more healthy life. Topics most suitable for groups are future trends for business, overcoming the competition, empowerment, quality management, or customer service.

McKenzie offers this advice on how to break into the professional ranks: "Become known. Write a book, seek opportunities to discuss your specialty on television and radio, write articles for business, meeting, and airline periodicals, and send out press releases to the news media whenever you're making a speech. Also, get listed in the *Yearbook of Experts, Authorities and Spokespersons."*

Authors often observe that it is ironic that writing just one book automatically seems to qualify the author as an after-dinner speaker. Program managers often think that anyone who has written a book should also be an interesting speaker. But, of course, that's not always the case. Authors may get a few initial bookings just because they are authors, but to continue in a speaking career, the author must make the jump from an ability to write to the separate ability to speak. They are different skills.

Once you've decided on your special niche, there is often a slow, plodding pace to professionalism. You begin by accepting invitations to speak to any and all audiences and groups seeking programs. Every local service club, alumni or professional group, church society, and retirement club is continually searching for a new program—*especially* if the speaker requires no honorarium. And there's the rub. When first starting out on the professional path, the first mile might be labeled "pro bono," or for a less elegant word, "free."

By accepting these invitations, however, you will be accomplishing two things: First, every person in those audiences becomes a potential reference for still another program. If you are good, they will say to others, "I heard this wonderful speaker recently; maybe we can get her [or him] to speak to our group as well." Second, during each of these engagements, you will be adding a bit more polish to both your delivery and your message.

Local Rotary, Lions, Optimists, and other service clubs are nurturing grounds for the aspiring professional. As a general policy, since they meet weekly, they cannot offer fees to their speakers, but they are usually wonderfully receptive audiences when a good program comes their way. Members of these clubs are also business leaders in the community, men and women who are often on the lookout for good speakers to appear before their sales force, professional group, or association.

Special Note: At this point, as you are doing these "freebies," whenever you finish delivering a program and you believed you performed well, be certain to ask the program manager: "If the program was satisfactory, would you mind providing a letter to that effect? As you know, such endorsement letters are very useful in reassuring other groups who are considering me." As these endorsement letters accumulate, they will serve that purpose beautifully.

This route could take several years, but it is likely that you will expand in ever-increasing geographic circles until one day some program manager will phone and say, "We would like you to speak, but we can only afford an honorarium of $100." Eureka! You have stepped up from the amateur's league to the pro level, albeit still a rookie.

Early in this passage to professionalism, you might learn if there is a local or regional professional speakers' association available to you. Twenty-six states, plus one chapter for the six New England states, and one each for the District of Columbia and the province of Ontario, Canada, have chartered speakers associations. (See the complete list on pages 189–192.) For nominal membership fees, these regional or state organizations offer opportunities to people who wish to improve and market their speaking skills. They may also provide advice and training on all aspects of professional speaking. Most meet monthly or bimonthly. Some even arrange for annual "showcases" where, for a fee, you audition before an audience of program chairpersons and meeting professionals.

MARKETING YOURSELF

As you venture forward into the field of professionalism, it is important to develop and produce certain sales materials that quickly and attractively describe you and your special credentials. McKenzie recommends that, if necessary, you enlist the aid of a graphic designer and writer to create a smart-looking leaflet, folio, or package that presents your special attributes. These materials should showcase such attractions as:

- Your experience in your special field.
- Copies of articles by or about you and your work.
- A short list of titles of your programs.
- Selected endorsement comments from program managers for whom you have spoken.
- A photograph.
- And, perhaps most important of all, a video "demo" tape that shows you at your platform best.

At this point, McKenzie suggests you may be ready to simultaneously approach a few speakers bureaus. Don't be disappointed if you are rejected or receive a cold shoulder, however. "The world is full of would-be speakers, both good and bad," she says. "With dozens of calls and letters arriving weekly, it is difficult to find time to review and respond promptly to inquiries." Most bureaus prefer to have heard you in person or receive a glowing recommendation from a client or another professional speaker before agreeing to represent you. Or, they may have read your book or article and are willing to take a risk that you might also be an effective speaker.

When a bureau asks to represent you *exclusively*, you've reached the loftiest speaker's platform position of all. Until then, it is the custom in the bureau profession to have nonexclusivity—meaning you can be listed simultaneously by several different bureaus. Also, as a free agent you can continue to generate and accept bookings directly, without involving any bureau.

ROLE OF A SPEAKERS BUREAU

Speakers bureaus operate this way: First, they serve a large list of clients consisting of associations, corporations, non-profit institutions, professional societies, universities, and colleges. Second, the bureau's income is derived mainly from commissions taken from the speaker's fee.

Fees are quoted by the bureaus as a "gross" figure, meaning that a commission is then deducted and the "net" remitted to the speaker.

Travel and accommodation expenses are almost always separate from the fee and are customarily paid for by the client. Some clients, especially colleges, want to pay all-inclusive fees. The client may also arrange for your air and hotel reservations, or request that you do it, then reimburse you later.

Once a speakers bureau has shown interest in you, follow up with a personal visit so that the bureau sales team can enthusiastically convince a client of your value. "A bureau's business is much like that of the old-fashioned matchmaker," McKenzie explains. "We put complementary qualifications together on both sides to achieve the perfect fit. And the more we know about the contenders, the better the match."

Once a bureau or agent makes a commitment to list you and begins to obtain speaking engagements for you, here are some typical services the bureau provides:

- Draw and issue the contractual agreement with the client who is hiring or booking you.
- Inform the client of your audio-visual and travel requirements, plus any other special needs.
- Provide you with detailed information about the organization, the event, and what is expected of you.
- Obtain a partial payment from the client in most cases, and retain that to discourage cancellation.

- Put you in direct contact with the client well before the date of your appearance so that you can respond more effectively to the client's interests and needs.

Of course, the bureau is also responsible for collecting the entire fee and sending you the net amount due within a reasonably short time after the engagement.

A representative of the bureau should also be in touch with you before the date of the engagement to obtain your arrival and departure times (for the client) and to assist you with any last-minute details.

After your speaking engagement, the bureau will follow up to make sure you were happy with the arrangements and to provide client feedback on your performance. This customarily consists of a written evaluation from the client.

In return, here (according to McKenzie) is what a bureau expects from you:

- Keep the bureau informed of changes in your career, such as newly published books or articles, current topics, or any other up-to-date information that will help them sell you.

- Don't inundate the bureau with unnecessary paper; the bureau does not want a postcard or letter every time you pack your bags for a speech.

- The bureau may even ask you to consider doing an occasional free engagement, perhaps to a group of association executives or professional meeting planners; both these groups represent potential future bookings for the bureau and you; they also usually pay travel and accommodation expenses.

- The bureau will expect you to supply your photograph, any marketing materials you can spare, and your tax identification number so that the bureau can file a W-2 statement with the Internal Revenue Service for all fees paid to you in the past taxable year.

FEES FOR PROFESSIONAL SPEAKERS

When starting out, fees follow the age-old economic truism of "what the market will bear." For example, a local retirees association may offer a token $50 payment, a small regional professional society might provide $100, and a small chamber of commerce might customarily pay its annual dinner speakers $500.

For an established speaker in, say, his or her home state, fees of $1,000 to $2,000 are not unreasonable. One speakers bureau president reported that "among all the speakers in the United States, from the Henry Kissingers who may demand $30,000 and more, to the newcomer who commands only a couple of hundred dollars, the *average fee* is $5,000. So, a speaker should not be afraid to move up the scale accordingly."

If you are commanding fees at the $2,000 to $3,000 level per engagement, that's when speaker bureaus begin to take interest and should enter the picture. They bring obvious benefits: They know the marketplace and can give you sound advice on how much to charge. They know each client and what they customarily pay to newcomers, experienced professionals, and celebrated names.

Speakers bureaus will charge you commissions ranging from 20 to 40 percent and sometimes more. Be wary of the bureau or agent who does not reveal the exact gross amount the client is paying for your services. Some speakers have reported situations where they learned—after the fact—that an agency had charged a client more than double the fee the speaker was actually paid.

The value of a bureau is obvious: They have hundreds, sometimes thousands of possible clients, and they can also negotiate a higher price for your talents than you may be able to obtain independently.

Most bureaus are also willing to cobroker with other agencies who have clients who want to book you for a program.

Another fee policy among many speakers involves "double-dip" programs. This may occur when you are booked for one engagement for, say, $2,000, and then the client asks if you will "double up" and do a separate presentation on the same date and at the same location. In this case, many speakers add a 50 percent uplift to their fee to cover the second program. Other speakers will negotiate a lesser amount with the rationalization that they are on the site and the extra time requirement is not troublesome.

Once you are along the road to professionalism, you face an important question: What do you say when the phone rings and the program manager asks the inevitable question, "What is your fee schedule?" At this juncture, you can either refer the inquirer to one of your speakers bureaus to negotiate the fee, or negotiate it yourself. Newcomers to the profession tend to be flexible about negotiating fees, whereas more established speakers have rigid fee scales.

Let's continue this scenario. You quote a figure and the caller responds with "Oh, that's a bit higher than we anticipated." In that case, the speaker can say, "Well, I know we all must operate within budgets. Do you mind if I ask what amount you have budgeted for a speaker?" Then, depending on the answer, the speaker must decide if it's worth the time and effort.

(The saddest scenario—for the speaker, at least—is when you quote a fee and the program manager says, "Oh, that's great! We expected it would be more.")

Speakers may possibly offer slightly reduced fees if the organization is nonprofit or educational. Distance and time also may affect a speaker's fees. For example, an engagement within easy driving distance may warrant one fee, but one involving a day or more of travel deserves a higher fee.

All these quandaries are eliminated, of course, if you use a speakers bureau to negotiate fees for you.

If you do both—that is, negotiate bookings yourself but also receive bookings from agencies—take care to stick to a fairly rigid fee scale lest you get caught undercutting fees being quoted by the bureaus.

THE NATIONAL SPEAKERS ASSOCIATION (NSA)

The NSA, which was formed in 1973, has its own Code of Professional Ethics and now counts some 3,800 members in the United States and other countries. Membership includes experienced professional speakers, developing professional speakers, vendors or suppliers to the speaking profession, and aspiring professional speakers.

Headquarters for this Association is located at 3877 North 7th Street No. 350, Phoenix, Arizona, 85014; the telephone number is 602-265-1001.

A membership directory is published regularly and is supplied to more than 8,000 "decision makers" who have the responsibility to plan and stage meetings. This directory features photos of members along with a description of their speaking subjects and, according to at least one speakers bureau head, is "a great advantage to be listed in."

There are three membership categories:

- *Regular.* All or a portion of an applicant's income is from at least 20 separate professional speaking engagements *for fee* each year.
- *Associate.* A portion of an applicant's income is derived from less than 20 professional speaking engagements *for fee* each year.
- *Vendor.* A supplier of services, material, or equipment to professional speakers.

Fees (as of 1992) for initiation are $175 (of which $100 is redeemable toward a future NSA workshop/convention within two years), and annual membership dues are $250.

The NSA also sponsors what it terms "Professional Emphasis Groups" or "PEGs." These groups are tailored to specialty subjects to allow professional speakers to share and learn on a focused basis. The PEGs meet regularly, have their own agendas, and are listed separately in the NSA directory.

The following PEGs currently exist:

Consultants	International
Educators	Sales Trainers
Health and Wellness	Seminar/Workshop Leaders
Humorists	Speakers Bureaus

Dues are $20 per group.

Membership in NSA brings multiple benefits to the professional speaker. It provides training and education, a directory to help you gain attention, and an opportunity to meet and mix regularly with others in the field.

Under a stiff set of criteria, NSA also awards the designation "Certified Speaking Professional" (CSP), which can be listed after your name on business cards, letterheads, and promotional material. The criteria to achieve this designation are as follows:

- Membership in NSA for 36 continuous months.
- A minimum of five consecutive years of professional speaking experience, during which:
  - A minimum of 250 presentations were given, with a minimum of 20 given in each 12-month period and for which a minimum fee was received.
  - A minimum of 100 different clients were served.
  - A minimum of 20 testimonial letters were received from clients served.
  - A minimum of 30 credit hours of professional education were earned at NSA conventions or workshops.

NSA also offers the following four insurance programs to members, their spouses, and key employees: major medical, disability income, catastrophe major medical, and term life.

OTHER GROUPS

Two associations are considered "buyers" of speaking talent, and it is wise to become aware of them.

The first is Meeting Planners International (MPI). This is a national association with many local chapters comprising members who have come to specialize in staging meetings. They can be independent agents or they can be employees of corporations—usually a large corporation that stages many meetings each year. In addition to negotiating for hotel rooms and meals, a professional meeting planner also books speakers and other forms of entertainment.

The second group of national importance is the American Society for Association Executives (ASAE). This also has many local chapters; chapters in New York, Washington, and Chicago are the most prominent because most national associations are based in those cities. The professional association executive bears the designation "Certified Association Executive" (CAE) and is constantly on the lookout for informative programs for his or her association.

In both of these cases, it is wise for the "wannabe" speaker to devise a way to speak before local chapters of both MPI or ASAE. The audiences of both could represent multiple bookings.

10

Resources for Help

**Locating reliable
speaking help
can be easy
and inexpensive.**

The Wall Street Journal reports that some speaking consultants may charge $1,000 per person for group counseling. Private assistance can cost even more. For example, a San Francisco trainer charges as much as $3,500 for a day of personalized tutoring. And other therapists, according to the *Journal*, even go so far as to prescribe *medications* to allow a client to withstand a "must" talk. Locating resources for help need not be that costly nor that drastic.

GENERAL SOURCES

Probably the single best place to start is with the Yellow Pages of your telephone directory. Look under the heading "Public Speaking Instruction." For example, the 1991–1992 Yellow Pages directory for Manhattan, New York, contained 18 listings for individuals or agencies that offered assistance; Greater Los Angeles had 5 listings; Atlanta, 10; San Francisco, 23. If your community offers such public-speaking instruction, sort through the listings and then phone to obtain more information.

A good example of one of these private training organizations is Frederick Knapp Associates, Inc., New York City. He and his staff traverse the United States offering executive seminars in major cities. Knapp offers four types of seminars: "Execu-Speak," which is a comprehensive two-day seminar devoted to all phases of business speaking, including the professional use of visual aids; "Execu-Speak, " an advanced two-day seminar on "final touches" for management presentation effectiveness; "Execu-Image," a two-day seminar focusing on improving total executive image and style; and "Media-Speak," a one-day course to prepare businesspeople for print, television, telephone, or crisis interviews. These seminars range in cost from $595 to $895 each. For more information, call 1-800-321-2299.

The next best source for assistance is probably your local library, where you'll find "how to" books on public speaking. In my local library, for example, there are some five dozen such books. Unfortunately, few were written especially for the businessperson. However, many of these books offer excellent *general advice* on improving public-speaking abilities.

The next most likely sources to examine are community colleges or vocational schools in your area. Many of these offer "how to" courses in basic public speaking. Moreover, they are offered on evenings and at other convenient times for busy businesspeople. As an example, classes may meet once or twice a week for a few hours over a span of 8 or 10 weeks. Nominal fees are usually charged. Be certain to ask if videotaping equipment is available as part of the training. In these classes, you will be expected to prepare and deliver short presentations to the class and before the camera.

In 26 states, the Washington, DC, and the New England areas, speakers' associations offer membership to people interested in improving public-speaking abilities. They often provide workshops and seminars on speaking and also on marketing yourself if you wish to begin speaking for fees. A list of these state-based organizations appears on page 189.

On the national level, two organizations—one nonprofit and the other an 80-year-old profit-making institution— provide excellent training grounds for the businessperson who wishes to gain practical experience.

TOASTMASTERS INTERNATIONAL

There are more than 7,000 Toastmasters clubs and 160,000 members in the United States, Canada, and 50 other countries, including two clubs in Moscow, Russia. Thousands of corporations and government agencies sponsor in-house Toastmasters clubs as training workshops for their employes. Clubs have even been established at military bases, colleges and universities, churches and prisons, as well as among senior citizens, professional groups, bilingual groups, singles, and the visually impaired.

Toastmasters was organized in 1903 in Santa Ana, California, by Ralph C. Smedley, a YMCA director who decided that older boys there would benefit from training in communications. This nonprofit organization bills itself as a club that fosters "learn-by-doing workshops in which men and women hone their skills in an atmosphere of fellowship and enjoyment."

The typical club has 20 to 40 members who meet once or twice a week to learn and to practice public-speaking techniques. The average club meeting lasts about an hour and a half. There is no single instructor in a Toastmasters club. Members evaluate each other's oral presentations. Each meeting features several members who deliver prepared speeches and are then evaluated by other members.

Members also give impromptu talks, develop listening skills, learn how to conduct meetings, and learn parliamentary procedures.

A new member of Toastmasters progresses through a series of 10 speaking assignments, each designed to instill a basic foundation in public speaking. Members then select from among 12 advanced programs geared to specific career needs. Those 12 programs are:

Public Relations	The Professional Speaker
Specialty Speeches	The Professional Salesperson
The Entertaining Speaker	Technical Presentations
Speaking to Inform	Communicating on TV
The Discussion Leader	Storytelling
Speeches by Management	Interpretive Reading

To obtain more information about Toastmasters International, write to PO Box 9052, Mission Viejo, CA 92690-7052, or phone 714-858-8255.

DALE CARNEGIE

The name Dale Carnegie has become synonymous with the phrase *How to Win Friends and Influence People* (Simon and Schuster, New York, 1981). That is the name of Carnegie's best-selling book, first copyrighted in 1936 and still selling after 15 million copies.

Dale Carnegie is also a registered trademark for a training program that is currently offered throughout the United States and 68 other countries. Unlike Toastmasters, this is a thriving, for-profit business that claims to train more than 170,000 men and women each year. According to the Carnegie organization, at least 9,000 companies use the Carnegie training programs every year, including 430 of the *Fortune 500* companies. Eight separate programs are offered, but the main ingredients in all of them are such things as how to improve human relationships, how to motivate yourself and others, how to build confidence in yourself and others, and how to become a better communicator.

Scattered across the United States and Canada are 88 licensed sponsors staffed by some 4,000 trained instructors. Active participation by each student in each class is an integral part of the Carnegie method. Cost, location, and frequency for the various Carnegie programs is determined locally, but tuition ranges from $750 to $1,500 (1991 rates), depending on the community. When in-house programs are offered, some or all of this cost may be subsidized by the employer.

11

Parting Advice from Successful Speakers

For this concluding chapter, I decided to turn to a dozen or more accomplished business speakers—people who were regarded as highly effective speakers by their peers. The purpose was to research answers to this question: *"What is the best, single piece of advice for someone in business who wants to improve his or her speaking skills?"*

Here are some answers to that question:

> I never spend time on the good parts of a performance; but I spend hours on the weak parts.
>
> *Cornelia Otis Skinner, Actress*

(On how to deal with the number one enemy, nervousness.)

> I've noticed that a great (golfer) like Lee Trevino yawns when he gets into a pressure situation on the course. It's a deliberate yawn that gives him extra oxygen and relieves tension. Under pressure your breathing becomes shallow. Yawning forces air into your lungs and to your brain. It's like taking deep breaths when you're nervous, only better.
>
> *Tom Watson, Golfing Star*

Be yourself. Be honest, direct, genuine. Immerse yourself in the facts, the arguments, the emotions. Then present it from yourself. Don't try to be something you're not.

Russell Spence, Trial Attorney

Always keep a record of every speech—what you said to whom and what worked and what didn't work.

Donald Field, University Associate Dean

Look for somebody in the audience you know or have met, preferably somebody sitting in the first two rows. If you can spot two or three such persons in the audience, all the better. Direct a remark or two to them during your talk. It might be a simple greeting or it might be something related to your talk. For example, "Larry, you've handled a problem similar to this last year." The point is that casual, personal remarks to someone you know in the audience can create a closer relationship between you and the entire audience. It also helps you develop better eye contact with individual persons in your audience.

President David L. Weiner, Marketing Agency

The best single piece of advice given to me (in my speaking career) was—Slow down! While it may have seemed cruel at the time, I was told that I was like a "wind-up doll" and when the key was turned on, I raced through my performance. I still suffer from that handicap and try to remind myself to change the pace occasionally.

Harry F. Franke, Attorney and Inveterate Emcee

Don't read a speech. Prepare an outline, rehearse privately, then wing it! Better to look the audience in the eyes and stumble a bit than to read a speech.

Dean R. Axtell, Chairman of the Board

Know your audience and know your subject. It's that easy. Then develop good eye contact and try to establish rapport with your audience.

Robert Brennan, Chamber of Commerce President

Know your subject. Care about your subject. And focus attention on your audience. The people who attend meetings are interested in you, your company, and they are customers—or potential customers. As a speaker, you're not only selling yourself, but the company you represent. Be informational. Describe problems and solutions. Everyone wants to share the solutions to vexing problems.

John Stollenwerk, President, Allen Edmonds Shoe Company

Know thy speech! Don't memorize it, but be so familiar with the content that only an occasional glance at the text or notes is required to keep you moving along the right track smoothly and naturally. In spite of butterflies—which are natural—this breeds confidence, which generates more relaxation, and I find the more relaxed I am the better the speech.

Alfred P. Diotte, Corporate Attorney

Know your facts . . . and then keep it light. Also, involve the audience by asking lots of questions to get them thinking and to keep them from sliding off their seats from boredom.

Robert Geffs, Bank Executive

What's the best, single piece of advice in business public speaking? The answer is one word: Rehearsing. I try to rehearse so much I can give the speech with confidence and seemingly extemporaneously.

Marsha Lindsay, Advertising Agency President

My piece of advice is to avoid the common practice of speakers who enthusiastically and bombastically tell audiences what they already know. It's called "BGO" . . . for the "Blinding Glimpse of the Obvious" syndrome.

Robert Milbourne, Business Association President

I have two bits of advice for aspiring business speakers. First, if you don't have the ability to open with a joke, don't do it! A joke that falls flat can unnerve the speaker as well as the audience. The second pieadvice is not to underestimate the intelligence of your audience. Simplify, but don't talk down with a haughty attitude of Mr. Know-It-All.

Daniel P. Meyers, Corporate Public Relations Executive

Know your audience very well. (1) Understand its mood, (2) determine, in advance, how informed its members are about your topic, (3) know its cultural/educational/ intellectual background, and (4) then try to stimulate its curiosity.

Carl A. Weigell, Company President

Finally . . . this concluding piece of advice appeared in *The Executive Speechwriter Newsletter:*

> If I went back to college again, I'd concentrate on two areas: Learning to write and to speak before an audience. Nothing in life is more important than the ability to communicate effectively.
>
> *Gerald L. Ford, President of the United States*

Local Chapters— National Speakers Association

State	Chapter	Contact
Alabama	Alabama Speakers Association Birmingham	Richard Brown (205) 578-4277
Arizona	Tempe	Joanne Winter (602) 277-1481
		Steve Tyra (602) 253-9055
California	Los Angeles	Ralph DiDonato (714) 661-8482
		Gayle Stewart (714) 832-1113
	San Francisco	Joanne Ryan (415) 994-1498
		Frederick Gilbert (415) 368-3699
	Sacramento	Bill Cole (916) 638-2706
	San Diego	Mary-Ellen Drummond (619) 756-4284

State	Chapter	Contact
Colorado	Denver	Suzanne Vaughan (303) 690-2300
		Voice Mail (303) 592-3770
District of Columbia	Washington, DC	David Alan Yoho, Jr. (703) 654-7070
		Voice Mail (301) 630-6605
Florida	Miami/Fort Lauderdale	Marlene Naylor (305) 821-5866
		George Chlamark (407) 688-0888
	Tampa	Sheryl Nicholson (813) 684-3076
Georgia	Atlanta	Terry Brock (404) 923-2800
Illinois	Chicago	Sam Lilly (708) 241-1515
		Joe O'Rourke (708) 541-4445
Kansas	Kansas City	Neita Geilker (816) 781-0973
Louisiana	New Orleans	Bob Gerold (504) 288-8241
Michigan	Ann Arbor	Julius Cohen (313) 429-4855
Minnesota	Minneapolis	Joan Kennedy (612) 780-8491
Missouri	St. Louis	Joe Ancona (314) 394-2019

State	Chapter	Contact
New England	Marlboro, MA	Margo Chevers (508) 695-8687
New York	New York City	Al Parinello (201) 784-0059
		Elaine Barbakoff (914) 234-7205
North and South Carolina	Carolinas	Benjamin Bailey (704) 333-7307
Ohio	Columbus	Beth Richardson (614) 221-1900
		Barb Wingfield (513) 468-2041
Oklahoma	Stroud	Larry James (800) 725-9223
Pennsylvania	Philadelphia	Carl T. Smith (609) 589-2629
Tennessee	Nashville	Al McCree (615) 370-0966
Texas	Dallas	Laurie Moore (214) 250-0633
	Houston	Sue Pistone (713) 481-6546
	South Texas	Ron Birk (512) 396-0767
Utah	Utah	Kathy Loveless (801) 363-1807
Washington	Nendels, Tukwila	Joe and Helen Hesketh (206) 562-0302
Wisconsin	Milwaukee	Chris Clarke-Epstein (715) 842-2467
		Ann Wells (414) 782-6788

Canada	Chapter	Contact
Ontario	Toronto	Steve Schklar (416) 849-5664
	Nova Scotia Halifax	Denis Cauvier (902) 883-7636

(*Note:* This list provided by and reprinted with the permission of the National Speakers Association, 3877 N. 7th Street, Suite 350, Phoenix, AZ 85014. Telephone (602) 265-1001. FAX (602) 265-7403.)

Additional Reading

Books on public speaking are plentiful as well as specialized, dealing with such subjects as persuasion, humor, oratory, speech writing, reducing fear, speaking in politics, general reference, and becoming a professional.

If you wish to do more reading, just head for your local library or bookstore. At the library, the general heading is "public speaking." In bookstores, books on public speaking are usually located in the section labeled "Reference" books.

The following is a list culled from both of these sources. The books are listed alphabetically by author:

Allen, Steve. *How to Make a Speech.* (New York: McGraw-Hill, 1986).

Alexander, Roy. *Power Speech: The Quickest Route to Business and Personal Success.* (New York: AMACOM, 1986).

Flesch, Rudolf. *The Art of Plain Talk.* (New York: Harper Brothers, 1946).

Hoff, Ron. *I Can See You Naked: A Fearless Guide to Making Great Presentations.* (Kansas City: Andrews and McMeel, 1988).

Iapoce, Michael. *A Funny Thing Happened on the Way to the Boardroom: Using Humor in Business Speaking.* (New York: Wiley, 1988).

Kushner, Malcolm. *The Light Touch: How to Use Humor for Business Success.* (New York: Simon and Schuster, 1990).

Kenny, Michael. *Presenting Yourself.* (New York: Wiley, 1982).

Lederer, Richard. *Anguished English.* (New York: Laurel, 1987).

Lederer, Richard. *Crazy English.* (New York: Pocket Books, 1989).

Linkletter, Art. *Public Speaking for Private People.* (Indianapolis: Bobbs-Merrill, 1981).

McMahon, Ed. *The Art of Public Speaking.* (New York: G.P. Putnams, 1986).

McManus, Ed and Bill Nicholas. *We're Roasting Harry Tuesday Night: How to Plan, Write, and Conduct the Business/Social Roast.* (Englewood Cliffs, NJ: Prentice-Hall, 1984).

Osgood, Charles. *Osgood on Speaking.* (New York: William Morrow, 1988).

Quick, John. *A Short Book on the Subject of Speaking.* (New York: McGraw-Hill, 1978).

Robinson, James W. *Better Speeches in Ten Simple Steps.* (Rocklin, CA: Prima, 1989).

Sarnoff, Dorothy with Gaylen Moore. *Never Be Nervous Again.* (New York: Crown, 1987).

Spinrad, Leonard and Thelma. *Speaker's Lifetime Library.* (West Nyack, NY: Parker, 1979).

Thomsett, Michael C. *The Little Black Book of Business Speaking.* (New York: AMACOM, 1989).

Valenti, Jack. *Speak Up with Confidence.* (New York: Morrow, 1982).

Zelko, Harold P. and Marjorie E. Zelko. *How to Make Speeches for All Occasions*. (Garden City, NY: Doubleday, 1971).

Zito, Arthur J. *"Unaccustomed as I Am . . ."*, An Executive's Guide to Public Speaking. (Fairfield, NJ: The Economics Press, 1963).

Index

A

Abramis, David, 85
Accents, 71
Ailes, Roger, 37
American Society for
    Association Executives, 177
Appearances:
    on TV, 131–147
    on videotape, 146
Aristotle, 17
Aslett, Don, 14
Association for Multi-Image
    (AMI), 107–108
Association for speakers, 168,
    175–177, 181
Audio-Visual equipment, 4,
    105–129
Audio-visual media, 110–112
Authors, as speakers, 168
Axtell, Dean R., 186

B

Barber, Red, 53
Believing, 15–17

Bernhardt, Sarah, 8
Berra, Yogi, 94
Bifocal glasses, 56
Body Language, on TV,
    138–139
Breathing, 9
Brennan, Robert, 186
Briefing books, 22

C

Capital Speakers Incorporated,
    10
Carnegie, Dale, 183
Certified Speaking Professional
    (CSP), 176
Chalkboards, 110
Charts, types of, 115
Churchill, Winston, 23–24, 40–41
Clocks, 45
Closings, 42–44
Clothing, for TV appearances,
    136–137
Communicators, great, 3
Computer-generated graphics,
    117

D

Dais, 66
Dale, Ron, 90
Davies, John, 15, 33, 66, 72
Diotte, Alfred P., 187
Dravecky, Dave, 166
Dreyfus, Lee Sherman, 39, 60, 167
Dry mouth, problems with, 71

E

Electronic presentations, 112
Emcee, serving as, 153–156
Execution, 21
Eye contact, 52, 67–69, 139–140

F

Fears, 8
Feedback, 76
Fees, 171–175
Field, Donald, 186
Flipcharts, 110–111, 115
Floyd, Robert, 14
Ford, Gerald L., 188
Fornwald, Mike, 5
Foster, Arthur W., 18–19
Franke, Harry F., 186
Fredericks, Alan, 156
Fright, stage, 9, 14

G

Geffs, Robert, 187
Gehrig, Lou, 10
Gestures, 16, 72–73, 140–141
    on TV, 140–141
Graham, Billy, 15, 73
Graphics, 106–129
Grover, Herbert J., 61

H

Haney, James C., 91
Headliner, the, 33–37
Holtz, Lou, 167
Holznecht, Richard W., 9
Horwitz, David, 135–147
Hostile questions, 142–144
Humor, 4, 83–103
    books on, 94
    examples, 95–103
    importance of timing, 90, 93
    international audiences, 161
    sources for, 87–89
    what makes it humorous, 87–91
    when not to use, 85–86

I

Iacocca, Lee, 15, 73
Iapoce, Michael, 91
Infante, Lindy, 88
Inkjet printers, 120
International audiences, 159–163

Interpreters, using, 161–163
Interviews, on TV, 141–146
Introductions, 150–153

J–K

Johnson Wax Co., 13
King, Stephen, 9
Knapp, Frederick, 133,
    135–136, 180
Kushner, Malcolm, 94

L

Laird, Melvin R., 55
Laser pointers, 126–127
Laughter, 71, 83–103
Lavalier microphones, 77
Lectern, 66, 75–79
Lederer, Richard, 94
Lindsay, Marsha, 17, 187
Logan, Serge E., 13

M

Makeup, for TV appearances,
    137
Master of ceremonies, serving
    as, 153–156
McKenzie, Phyllis Corbitt, 10,
    165–177
MediaPrompt Inc., 135
Meeting Planners
    International, 177
Memorizing speeches, 58
Meyers, Daniel P., 187

Microphones, 75–79
    lavalier, 77
    remote, 79
Milbourne, Robert, 187
Mirror, 18–20
Moderator, serving as, 153–156
Monotone, 70
Morris, Desmond, 73

N

National Speakers:
    chapter listing, 189–192
    information, 175–177
Nervousness, 136
Newhart, Bob, 2
News conferences, 144–146
Noonan, Peggy, 48, 50–51
Notes, use of, 58–63

O

Olivier, Sir Laurence, 8
Opaque projectors, 117–118
Opening, the, 37–42
Orben, Robert, 14, 38, 93
Organizing a speech, 33–44
Osgood, Charles, 36
Overhead projection, 117–118
Overhead transparencies,
    116–117

P

Pavoratti, Luciano, 9
Pen plotters, 120

Peterson, James R., 35
Physical aspects, 4
Podium, 66
Pointers, 127–128
Posture, 21, 73–75
   when sitting on TV, 138–139
   when standing on TV, 138
Practice, importance of, 3,
    17–23, 56
Preparation, step-by-step, 19
Presenters, 150–153
Professional:
   fees for, 171–175
   how to become, 165–177
   how to turn, 5, 165–178
   marketing yourself, 169–170
Projectors, slide, 75, 122–123

Q

Questions:
   answering hostile, 142–144
   four types, 144–146
   importance of, 26–33
   "Six Magic Questions," 31–33
Question-and-answer periods,
    156–159

R

Radio announcers, 52–53,
    56–57
Randall, Clarence B., 53–54
Reading a speech, 3, 19, 47–63
   aloud, 52–53
   how to, 56–58
   when to, 54-58

Rehearsing, 17, 23
Remote microphones, 79
Research, 11
Resources for help, 179–183
Rich, James H., 13
Room, the, 79–81, 127–128
Rush, William, 70–71
Russo, Thomas, 41
Ryan, David, 150

S

Sarnoff, Dorothy, 17
Schwarzkopf, Norman, 166
Scott, Willard, 8
Sherwood, Virginia, 141–144
Skinner, Cornelia Otis, 185
Slides, equipment for
    projecting, 118–119,
    122–123
Slides:
   types of, 118–119
   using, 105–129
Smedley, Ralph, 182
Smith, Roger, 26
Speakers bureaus, role of,
    171–172
Speechwriters, 48–53
Spence, Russell, 186
Stage fright, 9
Stollenwerk, John, 186–187
Summarizing, 43

T

Tape recorder, 18
Teleconferencing, 132

Television, 4
  announcers, 56–57
  interviews, 141–145
  appearing on, 131–147
Tension, 9
Thermal transfer printing, 120
Timing a speech, 44
Timing, value of, 11, 90
Toastmasters, 181–182
Tomlin, Lily, 8
Training for TV appearances,
  133–147
Transition statements, 41–42
True, Herb, 85

U–V

U.S. Chamber of Commerce,
  134–135
VCRs, 123–124
Video cameras, 21

Video projection equipment,
  124
Videos, 108
Videotape appearances, 146
Videotapes, 112, 123–124
Vinci, Vincent, 12
Visual aids, 113–125
Visual materials, 105–129
Visuals, production of, 115–124
Voice, 69–71

W–Y

Watson, Tom, 185
Weigell, Carl A., 187
Weiner, David L., 36, 186
Williams, Robert, 12, 46
Wright, Rudy, 160–161
Writing speeches, 48–53
Yeager, Chuck, 2